Battlefield Walks
KENT & SUSSEX

Battlefield Walks

KENT & SUSSEX

Rupert Matthews

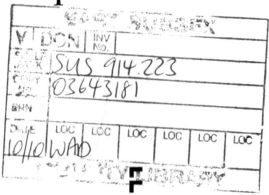

FRANCES LINCOLN LIMITED
PUBLISHERS

Frances Lincoln Ltd
4 Torriano Mews
Torriano Avenue
London NW5 2RZ
www.franceslincoln.com

A catalogue record for this book is available from
the British Library.

Printed and bound in China.

ISBN 13: 978-0-7112-2826-9

2 4 6 8 9 7 5 3 1

CONTENTS

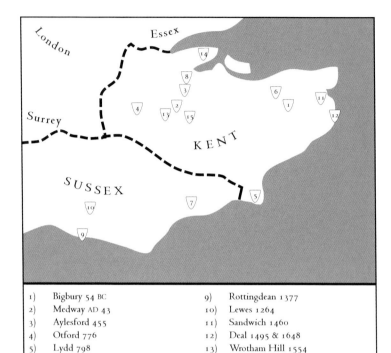

1)	Bigbury 54 BC	9)	Rottingdean 1377
2)	Medway AD 43	10)	Lewes 1264
3)	Aylesford 455	11)	Sandwich 1460
4)	Otford 776	12)	Deal 1495 & 1648
5)	Lydd 798	13)	Wrotham Hill 1554
6)	Canterbury 851	14)	Cooling Castle 1554
7)	Hastings 1066	15)	Maidstone 1648
8)	Rochester 1215, 1264 & 1667		

INTRODUCTION

As the closest areas of England to the continent of Europe, Kent and Sussex have long been a route favoured by invaders. The two counties have seen more than their fair share of fighting over the centuries. The Romans came this way, as did the English, the Normans and the French. Nor has the area been free of civil strife. Whether it was the medieval baronial wars, the Wars of the Roses or Tudor religious uprisings, the rich acres of Kent and Sussex have attracted both sides seeking an advantage over the other.

This book takes the reader on a journey through the military history of the two counties. It looks at fifteen of the more important battles and sieges to be fought out here, putting them in the historic context and explaining how and why the battles were fought. The book looks at the developing weaponry and tactical face of warfare and how this affected the decisions of the commanders and the outcome of the struggles.

Each battle is described in the course of a walk around the battlefield. Generally, though not always, the walk follows the route followed by one commander or unit during the battle. The text describes the route to be taken, and where to pause to inspect the points where actions took place and events happened. All the routes have been walked by the author or by Chris Coyle to whom great thanks are due.

Sadly, not all the battlefields of Kent and Sussex can be traced out on the ground. During the English Civil War, Royalist Arundel, for instance, was put under siege in 1643. The town held out for months before it was taken by storm in January 1648. The events, personalities and places involved are well known. However, none of the Civil War defences remain, the entire area having been built over since. Pevensey has a quite different problem. The Roman defences still stand here, but of the siege fought there in

491 all we know is that King Aelle of the Saxons captured the fortress from defending Britons.

Even when the site of a battle is known for certain problems still remain. The men fighting the battles had more important things to do than take careful notes about times and locations of individual events. All too often historical records are rather vague as to exactly where or when something happened. In writing this book I have tried hard to locate on the ground events as best I can. In the text I point out when a fact is known for certain, when it is probable and when it is merely conjectural. The maps of the battles should be viewed with this in mind.

This book has been a joy to research and to write. I must thank the good people of Kent and Sussex for the warm welcomes that they extended to me during my visits to the places mentioned, and to research facilities in the counties. I would also like to thank my wife for her patience.

I. BIGBURY
54 BC

Distance:	4 miles.
Terrain:	Mostly over well maintained footpaths or lanes. One section along the banks of the Great Stour can be muddy after rain. There is one short but steep hill up to Bigbury itself.
Public transport:	The walk starts and finishes at Chartham railway station.
Parking:	A small car park at Chartham railway station, and on-street parking in the village.
Refreshments:	The walk passes one pub, while a second pub and a general stores are to be found in Chartham, just off the route of the walk.

The Roman invasion of Britain in 55 BC is one of the most memorable dates in British history. In reality, however, it was no more than a scouting expedition. The real invasion and the serious fighting took place the following year in 54 BC. It was as part of that campaign that the Battle of Bigbury was fought.

For several years the Roman general and politician Julius Caesar had been fighting against the Celtic tribes of what was then Gaul, and is now France. By 56 BC he had subdued all of Gaul, either by outright conquest or by threatening the tribes into surrender. Caesar now found himself at the head of a large but idle army. Caesar needed at least one more impressive victory to keep his name popular with the Roman voters, and he needed something to keep his troops occupied. Seizing on the pretext of punishing those Celtic tribes in southern Britain who had helped the Celts of Gaul, Caesar decided to invade Britain.

The raids and reconnaissance missions of 55 BC convinced Caesar that the best place to strike would be Kent. This gave him the opportunity to defeat the local Cantium tribe before the larger Catuvellauni confederacy, based in Hertfordshire, could move south to intervene. He landed near Sandwich sometime late in June 54 BC.

It took Caesar several days to land his five legions, along with around 2,000 cavalry and some 10,000 light auxiliary infantry. Each legion was composed of heavily armoured infantry and, in theory, numbered around 4,000 men. Caesar's legions had been on campaign for more than four years, and we know he left detachments to guard key points in Gaul. He probably had around 12,000 legionaries with him when he landed in Britain.

The landings at Sandwich were unopposed. Caesar took time to build a wooden fortress near the beach to secure his base. He probably moved inland in early July, taking with him all his cavalry and auxiliaries, but leaving perhaps two or three thousand legionaries in the fortress under the command of his deputy commander Quintus Atrius. Thus it was with an army of about 10,000 legionaries, 2,000 cavalry and 10,000 light infantry that Caesar marched to invade Britain. He met the defending British in the Battle of Bigbury.

THE WALK

1. From Chartham railway station, walk south along High Street until you reach the parish church on your right. Just beyond the church the High Street crosses the Great Stour by way of a narrow bridge. Immediately before the bridge a small metal gate gives access to a footpath that runs along the north bank of the Great Stour. The path is surfaced with gravel and is clearly signposted as being the 'Stour Valley Walk'. If you continue over the bridge you will find the Artichoke Inn,

The church at Chartham lies beside the walk, just south of the railway station. It houses some interesting brasses and a fine timber roof, but was not here at the time of the battle.

Walk 1. Bigbury

which has a restaurant attached, and a shop selling snacks and cold drinks.

It was along this north bank of the Great Stour that the army of the Cantium tribe was ranged. Whoever commanded the Cantium in this battle – Caesar does not record his name – had obviously learned from the battles fought in Gaul. He knew that his Celtic

A Celtic chieftain. He wears an elaborate helmet that denotes his ability to command others. For weapons he carries a spear and shield, the standard weaponry of the period.

tribesmen were amateur warriors and would be no match for the professional Roman legionaries in open battle. Instead he had chosen to defend a river, backed by wooded hills topped by a hill-fort. It was a strong defensive position that the Cantium had good hopes of being able to hold at least for the few days that were needed before King Casivellaunus of the Catuvellauni arrived with his much larger army.

2. Continue along the footpath for about half a mile. You will then reach a private road which crosses the river by way of a brick bridge to reach Horton Farm. Go straight across the road, continuing along the Stour Valley Walk as it squeezes between the river on the right an old flooded gravel pit on the left.

Somewhere along this stretch of the walk there used to be a ford across the Great Stour. It was dredged out in the eighteenth century when the river was deepened to be able to carry canal barges and its

The Stour just east of Chartham. The river was dredged out and straightened about 200 years ago. At the time of the battle it was wider, marshier and crossed by a ford.

precise location is lost. It was at this lost ford that Caesar chose to force the passage of the Stour and get his army across.

Caesar used his elite 10th Legion to force the crossing. He ordered the men to adopt the formation know as the *testudo*, or tortoise. In this formation the men formed up in a dense column. The men at the front and flanks held their shields so that they overlapped, while those in the centre lifted their shields up to form a roof. The purpose was to provide protection against missile weapons, such as the light javelins with which the Britons were armed.

The 10th Legion moved down the slope from the Roman position on Larkey Hill, visible across the river. They crossed the ford seven men abreast while being pelted with javelins and sling stones and reached the north bank. Once across the river, the legionaries fanned out, pushing the more lightly armed Britons back. Gradually the Romans secured a large, semi-circular bridgehead which was rapidly filled with more legionaries marching down from Larkey Hill and crossing the ford.

After about two hours fighting, Caesar judged that he had enough men over the river to take the battle on to its next stage. He rode over the ford himself to take personal command of the critical break out stage.

3. Beyond the gravel pit, follow the signs for the Stour Valley Walk over a stile and into a large open meadow. This was probably typical of the whole area when the battle was fought. It was on damp pasture such as this that the next stage of the fighting took place.

As the Romans pushed north from the river they found themselves faced by the full might of the Cantium army. First into action and foremost in drama were the chariots. The chariot was highly prized by the Celts and was mentioned often and in awe-struck tones by Caesar and other Roman writers. Caesar wrote: 'The chariots of the Britons begin the fighting by charging over the battlefield. From them the warriors hurl javelins, though the noise of the wheels and the chariot teams are enough to throw any enemy into panic. The charioteers are very skilled. They can drive their teams down very steep slopes without losing control. Some warriors can run along the chariot pole, stand on the yoke and then dart back into the chariot.'

These showy chariots were reserved for Celtic tribal noblemen

A Roman legionnary of about 55 BC. He wears the mail shirt and carries the oval shield that were characteristic of this time. The short sword was used for stabbing at close quarters.

and kings, and they performed a vital role. The commanders and leading noblemen of both sides would gallop out in their chariots to career about the open space between the two armies. Racing at breakneck speed, the rival chariot warriors would indulge in all the flashiest and most visually impressive stunts they could devise. Typically the blustering warriors would taunt each other with insults and jeers, challenging each other to single combat or to races and deadly games. And while all this went on, the massed infantry would be singing their tribal war songs and indulging in chants of blood-thirsty intent or insulting language. Given the enormously colourful outfits worn by the Celts, and the banners and paint adopted when going to war, this must have been a dramatic sight and an exciting stage of the battle.

It was also crucial to the outcome of the coming battle for morale was at stake and this was the most important factor in the type of fluid fighting at which the Celts excelled. The army whose noblemen and heroes showed better horsemanship, handled their weapons better

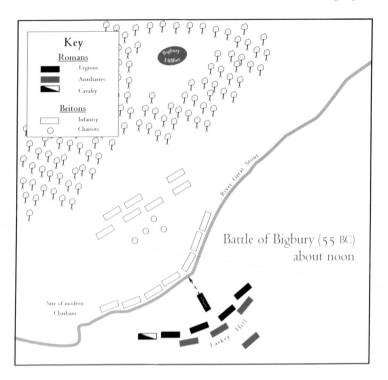

Key

Romans

Legions

Auxiliaries

Cavalry

Britons

Infantry

Chariots

Bigbury Hillfort

River Great Stour

Battle of Bigbury (55 BC)
about noon

Site of modern
Charham

Larkey Hill

or won single combats would have much higher morale than did the army whose charioteers had done badly. Before the main battle began one side would often have a clear superiority over the other. This might be enough to decide the battle. Certainly a dispirited force would be more likely to dissolve than one full of confidence.

It was this effect on morale that made the chariot absolutely crucial to the war effort of Celtic tribes in Britain. And also why the weapon was worse than useless against the Romans. The invaders did not go in for showy morale-boosting displays. All the finest exploits of the charioteers of the British were wasted. The Romans simply ordered their lines and prepared to start the killing.

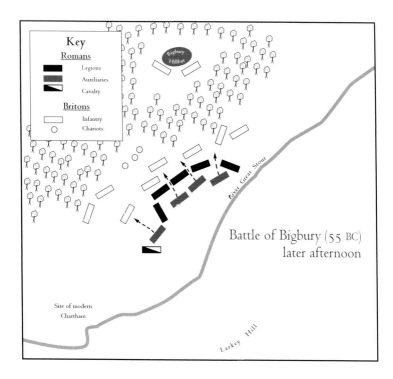

Battle of Bigbury (55 BC)
later afternoon

4. Continue along the river bank until the path crosses a stile to emerge on to the A28. Turn left along the pavement beside the A28 to cross a railway by way of a modern bridge. Just beyond the bridge, the A28 turns sharp left. A further 50 yards along the main road a lane turns off to the right, heading north. Walk up this lane for 100 yards, then turn right through an industrial estate to find a well-signposted bridleway, which is a continuation of the Stour Valley Walk. The bridleway runs through orchards and open fields for a mile before reaching a narrow lane close to Tonford Manor.

The entrance to the bridleway that carries the walk out of the small industrial estate. This route is well signed and the estate soon gives way to spreading Kent orchards.

These small apple trees form a spreading orchard that covers the ground where the Celtic chariots wheeled and charged during the battle.

△   Left: The lane that runs up the hill from the orchards towards Bigbury Camp hillfort. This is a dead end that leads only to a manor and a farm, so it has little in the way of traffic. Right: The unusual metal gate that gives access on to the stretch of the North Downs Way that runs beside Bigbury Camp.

▽   The North Downs Way runs around the northern edge of Bigbury Camp. The land around the Way is a nature reserve so walkers are encouraged not to stray from the path.

This stretch of countryside is where the main fighting of the battle continued. The chariots abandoned the field once it was obvious the Romans were unimpressed. The legions pushed forward in dense formations. When about 30 yards from the enemy, the legionaries halted to throw the javelins known as pilum. These had hardened steel tips and shanks made of soft iron. They bent on impact so that they could not be thrown back, and were designed to stick in a shield. The extra weight of the pilum embedded in a shield made it unwieldy in battle and tired the man holding it.

Then the legionaries moved rapidly forward to close with the enemy and go to work with their short, stabbing swords. Caesar tells us that this stage of the battle lasted much of the afternoon. The fighting must have been quite prolonged, although Caesar maintains that the issue was never in doubt. The Celts were gradually pushed back over this level ground toward the wooded hill to the north.

5. At the lane turn left, passing under a railway bridge to veer right as a lane comes in from the left.

Somewhere along this route, the Celtic army broke. The men started streaming north-west in defeat. Caesar halted his legions at about this spot, sending his light infantry in pursuit. Some of the legionaries were formed up into a firm line in case the enemy retreat might turn out to be a ruse, while others were put to work killing the enemy wounded and stripping the dead of anything valuable.

6. Continue along the lane, ignoring the turning on the left to reach another T-junction. Turn right. After about 150 yards, a curious metal gateway on the left gives access to a footpath

that plunges into a wooded area. This is the North Downs Way. Take this path. After about 150 yards the path reaches the humped mounds in the ground that are all that remain of Bigbury Hillfort.

The earthworks that defended this fort do not look very formidable after 2,000 years. They consist of a ditch around an earthen bank. At the time of the battle the ditch would have been deeper and the bank higher. The ramparts would have topped by a wooden palisade. The trees that today cover the site would then have been absent. The ramparts and their approaches were kept clear to provide a 'killing ground' for the slingers and javelin men who defended hillforts such as this.

The pursing light infantry were brought to a halt here. Many hundreds of the retreating Celtic warriors sought refuge inside Bigbury. As dusk drew on, Caesar brought up his heavily armed legionaries once again. The armoured men marched right up to the wooden palisade, which they felled with axes. Then the Romans poured into the fort. All the defenders were butchered, only a handful escaping to join their comrades in a headlong retreat to the north.

Caesar now unleashed his cavalry to pursue the enemy. It was, however, rapidly getting dark by this stage and before long the Roman horsemen called off the chase for fear of stumbling into an ambush in such unknown, enemy-infested territory.

Caesar and his army camped inside Bigbury Hillfort for the night. Next day a mixed detachment was left in the fort to guard the river crossing and care for the Roman wounded, while Caesar marched on to the north. The battle was over, but the campaign continued. Caesar would eventually meet the feared Catuvellauni north of the Thames.

The tumble down ramparts of Bigbury Camp are overgrown with dense woodland and, in places, can be difficult to trace.

The view north from the ramparts of Bigbury. The Celts retreated hastily across this land, now cut across by the traffic of the A2 which runs along the route of a Roman road built in around AD 43.

A typical Kent oasthouse marks the spot where the walk turns left to run downhill back to Chartham.

The view down to Chartham from the A28 to the north of the village. The walk crosses this busy A road on its return to the railway station.

7. Continue along the North Downs Way through dense woodland for more than a mile. Where the path emerges on to a lane, turn right, then almost immediately left at a crossroads, then very soon after turn right again. The Chapter Arms, which serves good home-cooked food, stands on this stretch of lane. Ignore a turning on the left and reach a T-junction. Turn left here to return to Chartham.

2. MEDWAY
AD 43

Distance:	5 miles.
Terrain:	Mostly over well maintained footpaths or lanes. One section along the banks of the Medway is often muddy and can require boots after rain.
Public Transport:	Burham is served by the Arriva 155 which runs between Rochester and Maidstone.
Parking:	On-street parking available at Burham.
Refreshments:	One pub near the top of Bluebell Hill.

In AD 43 the Roman emperor Claudius was in need of a success to bolster his rather shaky grip on power, then of only two years duration. When a British king named Verica arrived in Rome to ask for help in regaining the throne of the Atrebates, the tribe that ruled most of what is now Sussex, Claudius saw his chance.

After some preliminary diplomatic moves to ensure the neutrality of the Iceni and Coritani in the British midlands, Claudius ordered the invasion of Britain to proceed. Claudius gave command to the seasoned commander Aulus Plautius, then governor of Pannonia on the Danube. Plautius brought with him the 9th Legion Hispania, to which were added the 14th Legion Gemina and the 20th Legion Valeria, both from the German frontier. The expedition also included the II Augusta, commanded by the future emperor Vespasian. This gave Plautius around 20,000 legionnaires for his invasion. He also had a number of auxiliary units, though precise details of these have not survived. In all there were probably around 35,000 combat troops, plus a number of support and administrative personnel in the Roman invasion force.

A Roman legionary from the time of the invasion of Britain. He carries the oblong shield and wears the armour composed of metal strips that is most often associated with the Romans. The spear is a throwing pilum used to thin the enemy ranks as the battle began.

To face the invasion, the Britons had a mixed and divided force. The Cantium tribe, who inhabited Kent, had long standing links to Roman Gaul, but little wish to be ruled by Rome. North of the Thames was a powerful confederation of tribes led by King Caratacus of the Catuvellauni. It had been Caratacus who had ousted Verica and his removal from power was the pretext for the Roman invasion.

It is impossible to say for certain how many men King Caratacus could muster for war. The Catuvellauni themselves could probably field around 70,000 men, the Cantiaci around 20,000 and the Trinovantes of what is now Essex some 40,000. Undoubtedly other tribal allies could field some thousands of men, and just as certainly it would be impossible to gather all the men together at the same place and time. Cassio Dio, who wrote an account of the campaign, tells us the Romans were outnumbered. What is certain is that the vast majority of the Britons fought on foot. The famous chariots were manned by aristocrats who used them to travel at speed around the battlefield, but who usually dismounted to fight.

Having landed at Richborough, Plautius sent his fleet to occupy the harbour at Reculver while he marched his army to capture the tribal capital at Canterbury. Having crossed the Stour the Roman army marched along the North Downs with the aim of crossing the Thames to crush Caratacus and the Catuvellauni. The campaign had not begun until late in the summer and the Britons had dispersed to gather in the harvest. Despite this Caratacus moved quickly and managed to get a sizeable part of his forces gathered on the west bank of the Medway to contest the crossing and halt the Roman advance in its tracks.

Exactly where the Battle of the Medway took place is a matter of some controversy. The landscape has changed greatly since the first century, so the descriptions given by Dio are difficult to correlate to the scene today. However, it is generally thought that the battle took place where the North Downs are cut by the river, and the stretch of river at Burham Court fits the description given by Dio.

THE WALK

1. In Burham village walk east along the lane opposite Church Street. After a hundred yards this lane ends, but continues as a footpath that runs across open fields as it climbs up towards the crest of the North Downs. The path enters woodland, then climbs up a very steep section of chalk hill before emerging on to the summit of Bluebell Hill. The path emerges on to a surfaced lane beside the Robin Hood pub, which serves meals. Turn left to walk along the lane.

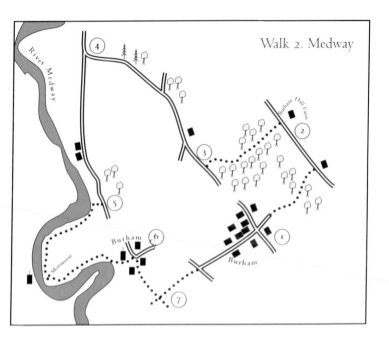

Walk 2. Medway

Undoubtedly Plautius would have used this vantage point, or one very similar, to size up the enemy and get an idea of the terrain over which he would fight. Looking west you will see the Medway running south to north in a series of looping bends a little under a mile away.

The Britons were drawn up on the far bank of the river on the level ground north of the church tower that can be seen on the far side of the river. There had been a narrow bridge over the river here, but it had been broken down by the Britons. Further south, to your left, there was a ford that could be used at low tide. Its precise position has been lost as the river has long since been dredged out, but it probably lay south of Burham Court, the small hamlet visible just this side of the river.

Left: The walk starts at this signpost that points uphill from Burham towards the crest of the Downs. Right: This pub sign marks the top of the hill. It was somewhere near here that the Roman commander stood to survey the British army spread out on the far side of the Medway to the west.

The bulk of the Roman forces were marched down off the hill to face the Britons across the Medway. This force consisted of three legions and most of the auxiliaries. One legion, the 2nd Augusta was sent south to occupy a position on the left flank.

The first move made by the Romans was to launch a diversionary attack in the north. For this Plautius used an auxiliary cohort recruited in Batavia, now part of the Netherlands. These men were drawn from a land of swamps and marshes. They were expert boatmen and were specially trained to be able to swim carrying weapons and armour.

2. At Burham Hill Farm leave the lane to take the footpath that enters the woodland to your left. This path passes along the left edge of the wood for about 150 yards before dropping down steeply off Bluebell Hill.

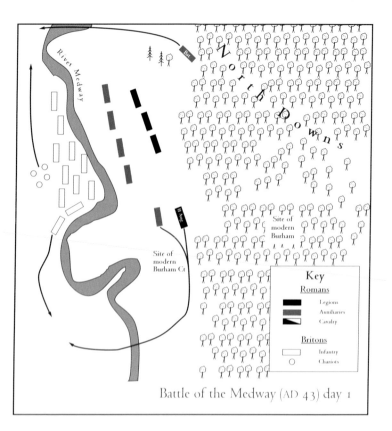

Battle of the Medway (AD 43) day 1

3. Near the bottom of the hill the path bends to the right, then leaves the woodland to cross a field before emerging on to a surfaced lane. Turn right.

The Batavian cohort moved north along approximately the route of this lane, though there is no evidence that the present road existed then. It was around noon by the time the Batavians had their orders. The purpose of the mission is not made clear by Dio, who describes

The walk follows the route taken by the Batavians along this lane towards the Medway River.

At this road junction the walk turns left. The Batavians advanced straight on to swim over the river downstream of the main British position.

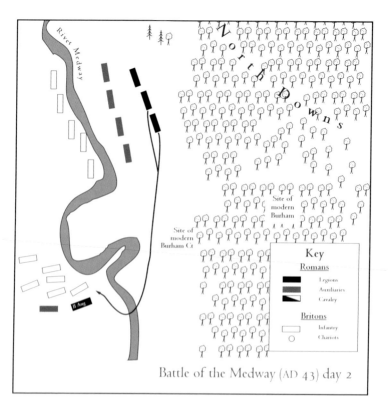

Battle of the Medway (AD 43) day 2

only the result. It is possible that they were intending to swim across the river out of sight of the Britons and then hurry north to block the tidal ford over the Thames at Tilbury and so cut off the Britons' retreat. If that was their intention, they did not achieve it.

4. Continue along the lane for over half a mile, ignoring the first turn to the left, but taking a second to the left where the main road bears to the right. The lane meets a T-junction beside some houses. Turn left.

The Batavians continued straight on across the marshy ground to the west and swam across the river. No sooner were they ashore on the far side than they were spotted by some British scouts. The fast-moving chariots came racing north to meet the threat. The key to the success of chariots on the battlefield was the mobility that they gave to the warriors who rode in them. The chariots would dash up to a perceived weakpoint, the warriors would leap down and surge forward to deliver a crushing charge. If that failed, they would run back, leap into the chariots and wheel away to seek out a new attack point.

The Batavians knew of these tactics, and while some formed a solid defensive wall, others hurled their javelins at the chariot ponies. This move was totally unexpected by the Britons. They drew back, saving their precious ponies and seeking instead to keep the Batavians pinned down until the British infantry could come up.

The bulk of the British infantry could not move as it was facing up to the main Roman force across the river. Some infantry may have moved north to support the chariot men, but not enough to drive the Batavians back into the Medway.

5. Walk along the lane for over half a mile as it gradually deteriorates to become a muddy track. Just beyond some industrial units an unsurfaced track runs right just before a surfaced lane turns left. Turn right here to follow the Medway Valley Walk along the banks of the river. This stretch of the river is flanked by marshy meadows and despire some drainage gives a good idea of the terrain that existed here at the time of the battle. About 450 yards along this riverside path you will find the modern monument to the battle and an information board. Continue along the path for another 350 yards. Just beyond a red river sign, turn left to enter the hamlet of Burham Court, passing to the right of the church before emerging on to a lane.

△ The River Medway at the point where the two armies confronted each other on the first day of battle. The British were to the left, the Romans to the right. The sheer drop down into the river at this point from the eastern bank can be clearly seen.

▷ This stone monument commemorates the Battle of the Medway, standing on the banks of the river alongside the route of the walk. An information board about the battle stands beside the monument.

△ The 2nd Legion probably crossed the
river about here, close to Burham Church
where modern industrial estates occupy
the west bank of the river.

▷ Leaving the river behind the walk
crosses the position of the 2nd Legion, then
takes this path across the fields to return to
the village centre.

Watching the events unfold from his vantage point, Plautius saw Caratacus' forces divide as first the chariots and then, perhaps, some infantry moved off north. The British army on the far bank still outnumbered his own, but Plautius seems to have reasoned that Caratacus must now have his attention divided between the main Roman army to his front and the Batavians to his left. It was time for the 2nd Augusta and Vespasian to move into action.

6. At Burham Court church turn right along a lane that runs almost due south. After some 300 yards the lane turns right, a track goes straight on and a footpath runs off to the left.

It was about here that Vespasian led the 2nd Augusta and an accompanying force of auxiliaries as they turned west to reach the ford that lay across the Medway hereabouts. Vespasian and his men got across the river in the later afternoon and very quickly came under attack from a force of Britons who had moved up river to face them. By the time the initial rush of Britons had been driven off it was dusk and fighting came to a halt.

The Romans were accustomed to their Celtic enemies retreating once a defensive position had been broken, so it was with some surprise and alarm that Vespasian awoke next day to find almost the entire mass of the British army bearing down on his isolated legion.

Back on the east bank of the river, Plautius saw the danger. He ordered his second in command, Gnaeus Hosidius Geta, to take two more legions across the ford to support Vespasian. The auxiliaries were left where they were, presumably to guard against an attempt by the Britons to cross the river.

Geta and his men got over the ford only just in time. The British attack had penetrated the defensive perimeter of the 2nd Augusta and in the confused fighting that ensued Geta and a handful of men were surrounded and cut off for a few minutes before being rescued. For quite some time the battle raged with ferocity but indecisively. Then as more and more Romans got over the ford they gradually came to gain an advantage.

Suddenly the Britons began to retreat, falling back northward down the left bank of the Medway. It was during this retreat the Caratacus first showed the genius that would mark his long struggle against the Roman invaders. While most of his men streamed north to pour across the Tilbury ford, it now being low tide, some of his most trusted warriors formed a rearguard. This force launched ambushes and shouted war cries to such an effect that the Roman advance was delayed until high tide.

The pursuing Romans were then lured into the treacherous Higham Marshes where they got hopelessly bogged down and became easy prey for the more lightly armed Britons. 'Many men were lost' recorded Dio of this incident.

The defeat of Caratacus by Plautius so late in the season marked the end of the first phase of the Roman conquest of Britain. The Emperor Claudius hurried north to cross the Channel in order to spend a few days in Britain and accept the surrender of various chieftains before riding back to Rome to bask in his triumph. Although south-eastern Britain had fallen to Rome, the west and north remained unsubdued. In particular Caratacus had refused to surrender and was to fight many more battles against the invader.

But the Romans were in Britain to stay. The Battle of Medway had ensured that.

7. Turn left along the footpath. This crosses open fields, passing under power lines. before emerging on to a surfaced lane. Go straight ahead and follow the lane back into Burham.

3. AYLESFORD
455

Distance:	4½ miles (or 1½ miles).
Terrain:	Partly over unsurfaced paths that cross open fields and meadows. They can be muddy after rain, but generally are fairly good. The shorter version of the walk is over footpaths. There is only one short, steep hill.
Public Transport:	Aylesford is served by main line railway and by several bus routes.
Parking:	On-street parking and a small car park available at Aylesford.
Refreshments:	Pubs in Aylesford, and a shop that sells snacks and soft drinks.

The medieval bridge over the Medway at Aylesford. The bridge is on the site of the ancient ford, which may have been passable only at low tide for the Medway is tidal up to this point.

The Battle of Aylesford was one of the most important and dramatic events in the history of Dark Age Britain. However, that period of history is not known as the Dark Ages or nothing, and details of events at the conflict are confused. Essentially there are two distinct versions of what happened here. This walk takes in the terrain relevant to both surviving versions.

In the year 410 the Roman Empire abandoned the province of Britain to its own devices. The Roman government and army were too busy with their own problems facing barbarian invasion to bother with the remote outpost of empire in the far north. At first the various layers of local government in Roman Britain carried on much as before, confident that the break with Rome was only temporary. By about 425, however, it had become clear to all that the Roman Empire was as good as finished. The local councils and rulers of Britain agreed to form a new independent government modelled on that of the decaying empire. There was to be a Senate of the richest and most influential men, which elected an Emperor to control the army and the day-to-day routine of government. This Emperor acquired the title of Vortigern, meaning 'high king', and may have been a nobleman named Vitalinus from Gloucester.

Whoever he was, Vortigern was faced by a crisis. The economy of post-Roman Britain was declining as its export markets collapsed, and the tribes of Ireland and the Picts were mounting increasingly serious raids. Vortigern's answer, endorsed by the Senate, was to hire one of the most famous mercenary commanders of northern Europe: Hengest.

Hengest arrived with his brother Horsa and some 300 men, generally called Saxons as they came from northern Germany. They were given the island of Thanet to live on and to serve as their base. So successful were Hengest and Horsa at driving off the Picts and Irish that Vortigern hired more Germanic mercenaries. The invaders were defeated and post-Roman Britain knew peace. The

Aylesford from the south bank of the Medway. The church stands on top of a small hill which may have been the site of a Roman settlement of some kind and almost certainly housed a Saxon farm at the time of the battle.

tranquillity would not last long. Many local councils and rulers began to resent paying taxes to the central government when they did not see that they were getting much in return.

Giving accurate dates for this period is difficult, but it seems to have been in 449 that the growing tension reached a head. Either unable or unwilling to pay, Vortigern stopped the supplies of gold and silver that were due to Hengest and his men. Hengest's response was swift and brutal. He led his men on a wide-ranging raid across Britain that saw the destruction of cities, the looting of villas and the slaughter of thousands. Hengest and Horsa retired to Kent with their spoils and declared themselves independent rulers.

Vortigern struck back in 455, sending his able sons Vortimer and Categirn to invade Kent at the head of a powerful army. They were met by the Saxons at Aylesford, where a Roman road crossed the Medway. This was probably the lowest ford on the river that could be used by carts, and so by an army with a supply train.

Just how large the army of the Romano-Britons was at Aylesford we do not know. It was probably no more than around 4,000 men given the size of contemporary armies elsewhere.

The majority of the army would have been lightly armoured infantry. These men typically carried a round wooden shield faced with leather that was about 3 feet across. They also wore a short-sleeved jerkin of toughened leather that had flaps hanging down to protect the groin and upper legs. Most would have had a leather helmet, though a few had metal helmets. The chief offensive weapon was a spear some eight feet long that was used to thrust at the enemy. Most men had a small axe or short sword to use if their spear broke.

The key striking force for the post-Roman British was the cavalry. There were relatively few such men in any army, rarely more than a hundred or so, but they were highly effective when launched in a compact charge. The typical cavalryman wore a short-sleeved tunic of mail that reached down to his knees. Most wore a helmet and all carried an oval shield about three feet by two. It is thought that these men used javelins, perhaps starting a battle with three or four such weapons which they would throw at the enemy before closing to use their long slashing swords.

The army that Vortimer and Categirn had come to fight was probably rather smaller. The Saxons fought exclusively on foot, though the richer men often rode to battle. The men used a thrusting spear as their main weapon, though every man would have had a heavy, single-bladed knife known as a scramasax as an emergency backup. Only the richer men would have carried a sword. For defence, the Saxons carried round shields rather larger than those of the Romano-Britons. The shields were covered with cowhide that had been specially treated to toughen it up. Most men wore

The Romano-Britons were equipped as were the later Roman legions. This man has a large oval shield and a thrusting spear. His armour is restricted to patches on his shoulders.

leather jackets of some kind, and richer men wore mail shirts. Helmets were common, with leather being the most usual material.

It is clear that Hengest and Horsa knew the Romano-Britons were coming, and equally obvious that they had chosen the place to halt the invasion with care. Both sides knew this would be a crucial battle and were determined to fight with grim resolve.

THE WALK

1. In Aylesford find the old medieval bridge over the Medway. Walk to the southern bank of the river.

According to the most widely accepted version of events, the battle of Aylesford began here. The landscape then was rather different from that to be seen today. The south side of the river is now dominated by the M20 and the main line railway, both of which race past a medieval friary, recently restored.

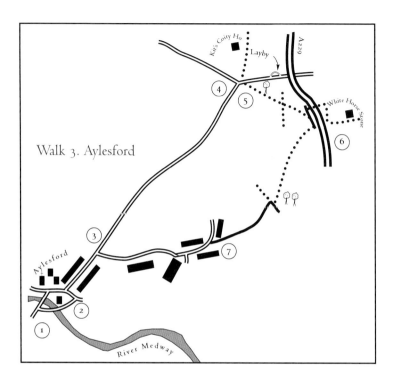

Walk 3. Aylesford

None of this was here in 455; instead there were broad open water meadows. Coming from the south, along roughly the route of the modern road, was the Roman road that the English called Pratling Street. This road ran down to the river, which it crossed by means of a ford. Roman fords of this type were usually improved by having a firm surface of stones or rammed chalk put down across the river bed and were typically some 30 feet or so wide.

Beyond the river stood a Roman inn or staging post that had been erected for the use of travellers. By this date it was probably occupied by the Saxon farmer Agaeles, who gave his name to the

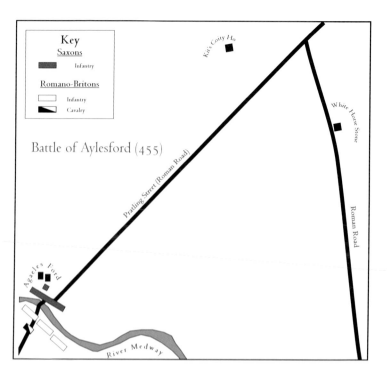

Key

Saxons

▬ Infantry

Romano-Britons

☐ Infantry

▰ Cavalry

Battle of Aylesford (455)

Kit's Coty Ho

White Horse Stone

Watling Street (Roman Road)

Roman Road

Agacles Ford

River Medway

place. The road then struck off north-east to climb up the escarp-ment of the North Downs and join the main army road running from London to Canterbury. A branch road ran off this main route, heading south to Maidstone.

The brothers Vortimer and Categirn most likely divided their army, with Categirn commanding the infantry and Vortimer the cavalry. Although the heavy cavalry were the most potent part of their army, the British brothers will have recognised that forcing a ford was no place for them. To be truly effective the cavalry needed space to manoeuvre, wheel and charge. A ford 30 feet wide would offer none of this. This was a job for the infantry.

No doubt this was why the Saxon brothers, Hengest and Horsa, had chosen to fight here. Protected by the river they would be secure from a cavalry charge. Furthermore the restricted front would give the advantage to the Saxons. Although the Romano-British had more men, they could only advance on a frontage of ten or so men at a time. The Saxons were semi-professional mercenaries accustomed to fighting and to warfare. At this date the Romano-Britons were more likely to have been conscripts than professionals. Man for man the Saxons were the better fighters. Although some spears and arrows could be hurled over the river, the bulk of the fighting would come down to hand-to-hand combat for control of the ford.

For their part the Saxons would have adopted the tactic that they called the scyldburh, but which modern historians call the shield-wall. This involved drawing up the army some six or so ranks deep with the better armed and equipped men at the front. The front rank then locked shields so that they overlapped considerably. This created a wall of wood and leather that had considerable resilience to assault. The weakness of this tactic was that it was remarkably difficult to move the formation in any direction other than forward or backward. If the need arose to move sideways or turn to face a flank, the formation tended to break up and then reform. This, of course, made it vulnerable to an attack based on flanking manoeuvre, and was another reason why the Saxons had chosen to fight at this ford where only a frontal assault was possible.

2. Walk over the medieval bridge, following the route of the leading Romano-British troops as they advanced over the ford. Walk up the slight slope to the parish church.

This slight eminence is where Hengest would have positioned himself with his bodyguard of elite warriors. The bulk of the Saxon force was between here and the river, blocking the exit from the ford.

As the Romano-Britons advanced they will have been met by a shower of javelins thrown by the more lightly armed men at the rear of the Saxon shieldwall. These will have caused some casualties, but the column pushed on to crash headlong into the front ranks of the Saxons.

The fighting at the ford was evidently long and fierce. Casualties on both sides were heavy. At some point in the struggle Horsa was killed, and so was Categirn. Eventually Vortimer ordered a halt to the assaults. He was losing men, had lost his brother and was gaining nothing. He probably spent some time eyeing the opposition before leading his men off along the Roman road to the south-west.

Such is the generally accepted version of events. However, another account of the conflict at Aylesford has come down to us. This puts the main action some distance to the north of the ford itself.

3. **You now have a choice as to how to proceed. You can either return to your car and drive, or you can walk to the next location. If you decide to drive, you want to head north up Rochester Road. Just beyond a crossroads and before passing under the main A229 dual carriageway there is a layby on the left. The car can be parked here. Then proceed on foot. Return along Rochester Road for a short distance to find a footpath on the right running uphill between trees to 'Kit's Coty House'.**

If proceeding on foot, leave the church east along High Street, then turn north along Rochester Road. This is a busy road so care will be needed as there is a pavement only along stretches. After climbing a hill a footpath goes left to Kit's Coty House beside a junction.

Kit's Coty House is the remains of a burial mound some 5,000 years old. Local tradition has it that the stalemate at the ford resulted in a single combat fought at this prominent landmark.

4. Turn up this path. The path is lined by hedges on both sides. After about 150 yards a gap in the hedge on the left gives access to a large open field in which stands the ancient standing stones known locally as Kit's Coty House.

According to the second account of the struggle at Aylesford, it was here that the main action took place. Arriving on the south bank of the Medway, the British brothers realised that they had little chance of getting across the river. Likewise, the Saxon brothers realised that while they could halt the enemy, they could not defeat him in a fashion decisive enough to end the war.

As a result it was agreed that Categirn would fight Horsa in single combat. The winner of the fight would become undisputed ruler of Kent. The place chosen for the combat was this ancient

The view across the Weald from Kit's Coty House. The ancient monument stands part way up Blue Bell Hill and offers scenic views in several directions.

stone monument. The standing stones visible today, and that were visible in 455, are the remnants of a burial chamber built around 5,000 years ago by the earliest farmers to plough the Kentish soil. The body, or bodies, to be buried were interred between the stones and a mound of earth piled on top. The earth has gone, but the stones remain. Perhaps their age lent them some mystic significance that made them an ideal venue for the single combat.

Whatever the reason, the fight between Horsa and Categirn took place here in front of the personal retinues of the two men. The result was the same as that recorded in the other version of the battle. Both men were killed, and Vortimer retreated from the ford.

Whichever version of events represents the truth, the aftermath of the battle is undisputed. Hengest grieved for his brother and decided to give him a burial fit and proper for a warrior-prince and devotee of the pagan gods. The body was lifted up and carried.

The Pilgrim's Way is a relatively broad and well trodden footpath that runs along the Downs toward Canterbury. This is the stretch between Kit's Coty House and the A229.

The White Horse Stone marks the traditional burial spot of Horsa, brother of Hengest and the most famed Saxon warrior of his generation.

Follow the route of the burial procession.

5. Return back down the hill to the lane. Cross straight over and take the Pilgrim's Way. This track crosses a second, then meets a stretch of derelict tarmaced road, which is the old A229. Turn left, then after just 50 yards turn right to pass under the thundering traffic of the A229 dual carriageway by means of a concrete tunnel. On the far side bear right to pass a petrol station on your right, then turn left to cross a footbridge over the railway. Continue up the main footpath between trees. After about 50 yards you will find a standing stone beside the path on the left. This is the White Horse Stone.

This is the spot where Horsa was buried. Sacrifices were made and a feast consumed as the mangled body of the warrior was laid to rest. The stone was then erected over the grave. As a final tribute Hengest had the stone painted blood red, and then on the red he drew the design of a white horse, perhaps to symbolise the magical horse on which the war god Woden rode out over the world to collect warriors to join him in his feasting hall. The white horse on a red field would become, and remains to this day, the symbol of Kent.

The clash at Aylesford, whatever form it took, was of enormous importance to the future history of Britain. The failure of Vortimer and Categirn to drive the Saxons out of Kent ensured that the barbarians had gained a secure foothold in the island of Britain. Hengest sent back to Germany for more warriors and settlers to come to help him hold and expand his new kingdom. Some came to Kent, others landed elsewhere along the eastern coast of Britain.

In time these mixed groups of Germanic invaders and settlers became the English. They would conquer most of lowland Britain and turn it into England. The surviving Roman culture of Britain crashed into oblivion and the surviving Romano-Britons became the Welsh, hemmed into their mountainous land to the west.

If the brothers Vortimer and Categirn had only got across the Medway at Aylesford it would all have been very, very different.

6. If you drove here from Aylesford, return to your car the way you came and so finish the walk. To walk back to Aylesford, return under the A229 and turn left along the derelict road. Instead of turning right back to Kit's Coty House, go straight on a short distance and then join a footpath that strikes off south-west over open fields towards an orchard about half a mile away. Just beyond the orchard the path meets a farm

The walking route back to Aylesford from White Horse Stone passes over fields and past a traditional oasthouse.

track. Bear right, following the track past a farm and oasthouse to continue south-west.

7. This track eventually meets a surfaced lane. Turn left. Follow this lane, passing an industrial estate on the left, to a T-junction. Turn left to return to Aylesford.

4. OTFORD
776

Distance:	1¾ miles
Terrain:	Mostly over unsurfaced paths that cross open fields and meadows. They can be muddy, but generally are fairly good. There are no steep hills or otherwise difficult terrain.
Public Transport:	Otford is served by main line railway and by Arriva bus 421 from Sevenoaks.
Parking:	On-street parking available at Otford.
Refreshments:	A pub in Otford, and a shop that sells snacks and soft drinks.

For some centuries after the Battle at Aylesford, Kent retained its status as an independent kingdom. For a while it was the richest and most powerful of all the various kingdoms in England, but by the later eighth century Kent was in decline. Other English kingdoms had established trade links with the continent, undermining the monopoly that had been the basis of Kentish wealth. The line of descendants from Hengest had produced a succession of short-lived and weak kings. Then, in 765 Egbert came to the throne. And Egbert was not a man to take insults easily.

By the time Egbert came to the throne, Kent had come under the domination of King Offa of Mercia. The exact nature of this over-lordship is unclear, but we know that in 764 Offa travelled to Canterbury to meet the Archbishop of Canterbury and acted as arbiter in some complex land disputes. The then king of Kent, Heahbert, seems to have accepted Offa's decisions as being the Mercian king's right, rather than a favour or privilege.

A few weeks after Egbert inherited the kingdom he granted some royal lands to the Bishop of Rochester. Offa wrote saying that he

▷ The walk starts at this signpost that indicates the path to be taken off the main road, heading north along the banks of the Darent.

▽ The main fighting during the Battle of Otford probably took place here where a modern bridge carries the road over the Darent at the spot where a ford existed in medieval times.

approved, though it is unclear if either Egbert or the bishop had asked him for his opinion. The relationship between Offa and Egbert seems to have remained tensely polite for some years. Then, in 774, Offa gave some land that he owned in Kent to the Archbishop of Canterbury without first seeking the approval of the King of Kent, as he should have done. Egbert protested, Offa ignored him.

The dispute broke out into open warfare in 776. We don't know exactly what sparked the war, but it may have been a new dispute over the right of Egbert to have authority in his own kingdom without reference to Offa. Archbishop Janbert backed Egbert's position with the full weight of his considerable ecclesiastical authority. The Kentish king also seems to have been related to the royal family of Wessex, which lent him help of some kind. At this time a vision was seen in the heavens of Christ's cross bathed in blood. Nobody knew quite what it meant, but few thought it a good omen.

When he received news of Egbert's assertion of full independence, Offa moved quickly. He sent an army marching south to London with orders to kill or capture Egbert and bring Kent to heel. We do not know the name of the Mercian commander, but his army passed over London bridge without incident, then swung south-east to enter Kent by crossing the River Darent at the ford at Otford. Perhaps the crossing at Dartford was guarded or considered too obvious a route.

The army sent by Offa does not seem to have been particularly large by the standards of the day – perhaps around 3,000 men or so. The men who made up this army fought exclusively on foot, though many men rode horses or ponies on the march. The richer men and their retainers would have been equipped with mail shirts that reached to the thighs and would have worn metal helmets. The poorer men lacked such metal armour and would have worn jackets and hats of toughened cowhide, if they could afford any armour at

An English warrior from the time of Otford. He carries a large round shield and a spear. The sword marks him out as being a man of some wealth.

all. The main defensive equipment for all men was the round shield. This was about three feet across and made of lime wood over which was stretched toughened hide. The lime wood was chosen as it had the ability to close on and grip any object, such as an arrow, that penetrated it. The enveloping leather gave form and structure to the shield, holding in place the various strips of wood that made up the body of the piece.

The chief offensive weapon at this time was the heavy thrusting spear. This was typically about 8 feet long and topped by an iron, broad-bladed spearpoint. Most men carried a knife or small axe as a side weapon to use if the spear broke. A few men may have carried swords, but these were prestige weapons owned only by wealthier men. Equally small numbers of men would have brought along hunting bows to shoot arrows at the enemy, but these were always a minority weapon.

The main tactic at the time was the shieldwall. This involved the front ranks closing up and locking shields to produce a solid wall of timber that was proof against incoming arrows. The force formed up behind this wall some six or so ranks deep, then advanced on the enemy. It was usual to place the more experienced men at the front to ensure that the face of the formation remained tightly knit and as straight as possible. It is thought that formations usually advanced at a trot so as to combine momentum with the ability to keep formation. Once the two sides were locked in combat, it was a matter of spear thrusts and counter thrusts to kill and injure the opposition. Eventually one side or other would begin to lose formation, and often the shieldwall broke up completely as an army turned in rout.

The Kentish army holding the ford at Otford was armed and equipped in a similar fashion to the Mercian force advancing against them. Again, it was not a particularly large army but it may have been slightly larger than that of the invaders.

THE WALK

1. In Otford find the more westerly of the two bridges over the Darent.

The exact position of the old ford is now not known, though it was certainly within fifty feet or so of the modern bridge. For the Mercians to penetrate far in to Kent they needed to secure control of this crossing point.

The reason for the ford's importance was that the Mercian men had with them a considerable supply train. Operating a hundred or more miles away from home meant that the men had to bring with them supplies of food as well as camping and cooking equipment. The loads might have been carried on pack horses or on carts, but in either case a good ford was needed if the equipment was to be got over the Darent in good condition.

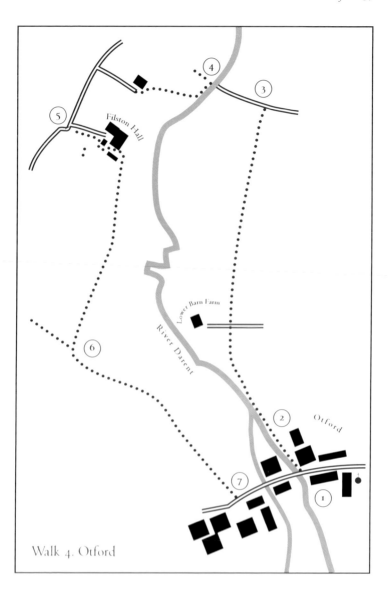

Walk 4. Otford

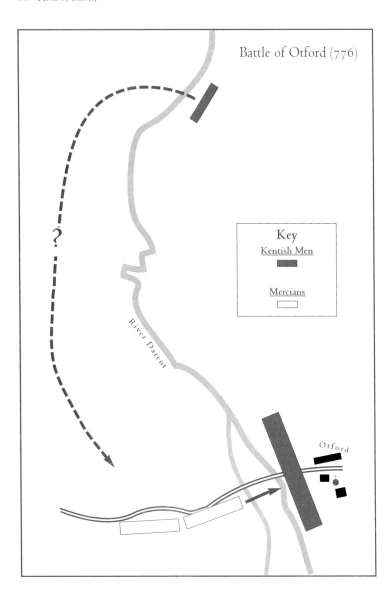

Battle of Otford (776)

Key

Kentish Men

Mercians

River Darent

Otford

To hold the ford, Egbert would have arrayed his army on this eastern bank, with its centre focussed on the ford itself. If he placed his main force actually on the river bank it was unlikely that the Mercians would have been able to force their way over. To fight effectively the Mercians needed good, secure footing. The only part of the river that offered this was the ford itself, and that was so narrow that only a few men could advance abreast. It would have been possible for men to get over the river on either side of the ford, but they would have been at a severe disadvantage when trying to get out of the water on the far side.

However, Egbert must have known that merely halting the invasion at Otford would not be enough. The Mercians had the choice of a number of crossing points into Kent, and indeed could have marched south to get around the river altogether. Unless Egbert was lucky he might end up guarding the wrong ford and find himself attacked from the rear. If Egbert was to make Kent's independence from Mercia mean anything, he had to defeat the invading army so thoroughly that Offa would think twice before sending another.

One option open to Egbert was to place his main army further back, perhaps about where the church now stands. This was the site of the old village, which would have allowed him to hide at least some of his troops out of sight of the Mercians. It might then have been possible to allow the Mercians to begin crossing the river before attacking. Those Mercians on the east bank of the river would be caught by surprise and be heavily outnumbered by the men of Kent. They might be slaughtered with comparative ease before the remainder of the Mercians could get over the river to help.

However, Egbert had another option, and another worry, due to the nature of the River Darent a mile or so to the north.

2. Immediately beside the eastern bridge a short driveway gives access to some houses and industrial units. Follow this drive to

▷ From Otford itself the walk passes through this kissing gate to enter open fields and head north toward the smaller ford where the Kentish ambushing force may have crossed the river.

▽ The old stone waymarker that marks the spot where the footpath over the fields meets the surfaced lane to the ford. Although the arrow points right, the walk goes to the left.

its end, where a footpath continues northward over fields on the east bank of the Darent. As the path bends away from the river bank it crosses over the lane that gives access to **Lower Barn Farm**. Go straight over the lane and continue along the path.

This area of water meadows to the north of Otford have not been greatly altered over the years. The pasture has been improved, but otherwise the damp grassland is much as it was back in 776. This stretch of land gives a very clear idea of what the battlefield would have looked like in 776.

3. Where the path emerges on to a surfaced lane, turn left. Follow the lane to where it ends at the River Darent.

The crossing here is a modern footbridge and ford, though the latter is not really useable by motor vehicles, but there is evidence that there was a small ford here before the bridge was built. It was not a regular ford, such as that at Otford, but would probably have been passable by horsemen. Whatever the nature of the crossing, it posed a problem and an opportunity to King Egbert.

If the Mercians knew about the crossing and put men over it, they would have been able to march south to attack the Kentish army on its right flank. Similarly, a Kentish force put over the river here could have attacked the Mercians on their left flank. Being on home ground, Egbert would have known of any possible crossing points such as this, but being far from familiar territory the Mercians might have been aware only of the formal crossing at Otford. Either way, it would have made sense for Egbert to put a force of men here.

It is clear that the Mercians did not know of the crossing, or if they did made no effort to use it. Egbert's flanking force was there-

The pedestrian bridge that crosses the Darent at the northern ford. This view is taken looking to the east.

fore free to cross to the western bank and march south to launch a flank attack on the Mercians just as their attention was firmly fixed on trying to batter a path across the ford at Otford.

4. At the far end of the bridge, the footpath divides. Take the left hand fork that runs alongside the river. This leads to a farm. At the farm turn right on to a drive that leads to a surfaced lane. Turn left down this lane.

5. After 200 yards or so, turn left again on the lane that leads to Filston Hall. There are two parallel lanes, the right hand one is the public right of way. Where this path meets a barn, turn right to skirt around the barn, then bear left to enter a farmyard and continue straight on to pass between outbuildings. Beyond the buildings an unsurfaced lane turns right. After 300 yards or so this track runs out on open fields to become a footpath.

6. Where this footpath meets another in front of some trees, turn left. This path runs up the left bank of the Darent to arrive on the road through Otford some distance west of the bridge, or ford as it was in 776.

If the Kentish flanking force did cross the river and march south, this is where they would have run into the Mercian army. Whether Egbert did send out a flanking force, or lured part of the enemy over the river to be ambushed, he achieved a quite startling victory. The Mercian army sustained heavy casualties and fled back towards London and safety.

7. Continue east along Otford High Street to cross the Darent and return to the start point.

The path that runs south along the west bank of the Darent. It was probably along this route that the ambushing force of Kent men advanced. The road along which the Mercians were advancing lies just beyond the line of trees.

It was from here that King Egbert of Kent was able to view the defeated Mercians streaming westwards. By winning the Battle of Otford in convincing fashion he made a reality of Kent's independence as a kingdom. We do not know how long Egbert lived after this momentous battle, but by 784 he had been succeeded by King Elmund, who seems to have been a cousin of some kind.

Offa of Mercia had not forgotten about Kent. As events were to prove, he was merely biding his time and waiting for an opportunity to strike.

5. LYDD
798

Distance:	5½ miles
Terrain:	Mostly over surfaced lanes or gravel tracks. The land around Lydd is flat and offers no serious obstacles.
Public Transport:	Stagecoach bus route 711 from Hastings to Hythe.
Parking:	On-street parking available at Lydd.
Refreshments:	Several pubs in Lydd, and two shops in the High Street that sell snacks and soft drinks.

After his victory at Otford, King Egbert of Kent was able to enjoy the independence of his kingdom for the rest of his life. His successors were not so lucky.

By 785 King Elmund of Kent had been persuaded, presumably by the threat of Mercian military might, to acknowledge King Offa as his overlord. Offa soon tightened his grip. He began to insist that the King of Kent could not enact any law nor grant any land unless the King of Mercia agreed first.

In the spring of 796 Kent gained a new king in the shape of King Edbrit Praen. Quite how he was related to Elmund, Egbert or the previous kings is unknown as the contemporary chroniclers do not bother to record this detail. There is some indication, however, that he was not the legitimate heir. Perhaps the true heir was a babe in arms, in exile or otherwise unavailable to sit on the throne.

Wherever he came from, Edbrit Praen was clearly not a man to laze about. Within weeks of coming to the throne he heard that King Offa of Mercia was on his deathbed. Praen decided to match the example of Egbert. He declared Kent to be fully independent of Mercia and refused entry to Offa's men. When Offa died he was succeeded by his son Egferth, who promptly fell ill and died a few months later. It was

◁ The church at Lydd is widely known as the Cathedral of the Marsh and is the largest church in Kent after Canterbury Cathedral. The tower is largely fifteenth century and, when open, offers stunning views across Romney Marsh. The body of Lydd church retains some Saxon work that may date to only a few years after the battle. The church was badly damaged by bombs during the Second World War – the nearby Lydd Airport was then an RAF base – but it has now been fully restored.

▽ Looking north along the B2075. The original causeway through the marshes ran along this route and it was most likely at about this spot that the fighting took place.

Praen's misfortune that another death that year was that of Archbishop Janbert. This supporter of Kentish independence also passed away to be replaced by Archbishop Athelhard, a Mercian.

With Egferth dying, the Mercians were too busy deciding on a new king to take much notice of events in Kent. But by the spring of 798 the new ruler, King Cenwulf, was securely on the throne and determined to prove his power. That meant subduing Kent. Unlike Offa in 776, Cenwulf was marching to Kent himself with the full might of Mercia marching with him.

The army that Cenwulf led into Kent was a large one, though we have no precise figures it probably numbered some 10,000 men. Praen could not hope to match such a force in open battle, so he did not even try. Instead he fled into hiding. He knew that keeping such a large army in the field was expensive in terms of both money and prestige. Before long the Mercians would be needed elsewhere, or would have to return home to the harvest. If Praen could elude Cenwulf he might yet emerge with some degree of authority intact.

It was not to be. Some time in midsummer Cenwulf learned that Praen was hiding with a few select men in Romney Marsh, almost certainly on the island of Lydd. Sending some of his men off to harry lands belonging to Praen, Cenwulf marched south by way of Ashford to the watery wastes of the marsh.

THE WALK

1. In Lydd find the parish church. This marks the centre of the old island of Lydd.

Lydd church had to be restored after sustaining bomb damage in the Second World War, but even so some elements of the old English church remain. These seem to date from about a century

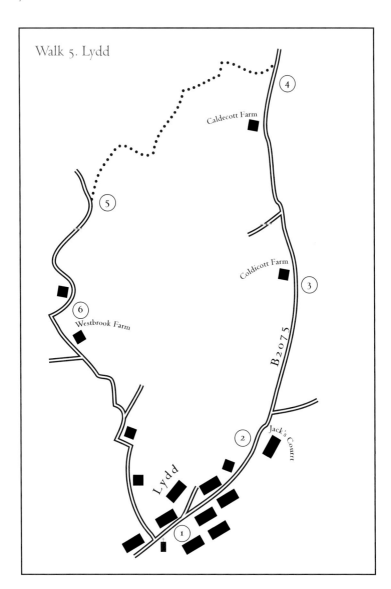

Walk 5. Lydd

after the Battle of Lydd, but undoubtedly they stand on the site of the wooden church that served Lydd on the day of the battle. It was here that King Edbrit Praen prayed before going out to fight. The tower is occasionally open to the public, and gives magnificent views out across the marsh and the area where the battle was fought.

2. Leave the church and head north-west up Station Road. After about 600 yards the road leaves the town and emerges on to the windswept Romney Marsh beside Jack's Court, the site of the medieval manor house.

Until the eighteenth century, Romney Marsh really was a marsh. What are today flat pasture lands dotted with grazing sheep were then bogs and reedbeds interspersed with stretches of open water and stagnant pools. There were paths through the marsh, but they were few and treacherous. A shower of rain could cause them to vanish into the mud for days on end. Only an experienced marshman could hope to find his way through these wastes with confidence. No wonder Praen had chosen to hide out on Lydd.

Precisely how Lydd was connected through the marshes to the next island at Romney in 798 we do not know. It is most likely, however, that the path through the dismal meres followed the route of the medieval causeway, now the B2075.

Praen will have known that Cenwulf was approaching and that he was most likely to come along the causeway. Praen had nowhere left to run. Sussex was allied to Mercia, as was the kingdom of the Franks beyond the Channel. To meet the advancing Mercians, Praen would have tried to block the causeway, relying on the impassable nature of the surrounding marshes to protect his flanks and rear.

3. Continue north along the B2075. Pause at the turning on the left to Coldicott Farm.

Battle of Romney Marsh (798)

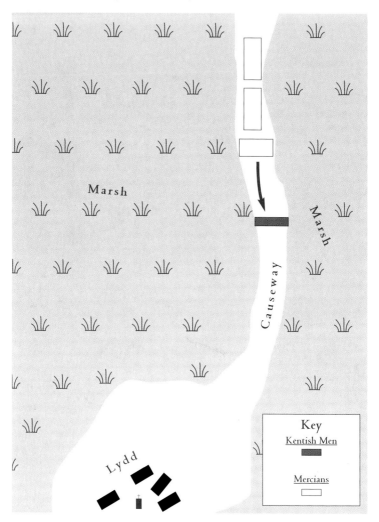

It was somewhere here that the fighting took place. It must be assumed that Praen formed his men up into the shieldwall formation to block the causeway, while Cenwulf adopted the same formation for his much larger force. The shieldwall is often thought of as being a tactic adapted to static defence, but it could also be highly effective in attack.

Once formed up in a dense mass with interlocked shields facing the enemy, the infantry would begin to advance at a walk. The more experienced men in the front rank would continually be seeking to keep the line as straight as possible, making sure the shields were interlocked effectively. If the commander felt confident in his men's ability to keep formation he would order them into a jogging run as they approached the enemy. This built up a momentum which, if the formation held tightly together, could be unstoppable.

If Cenwulf did lead his men forward at the run it might explain the collapse of Praen's defence. The Kentish line crumpled, broke up and collapsed. Praen himself was grabbed as he tried to get away. Most of his men fled into the marsh, hoping to find some path to safety to escape the stabbing spears of the Mercians. How many of them escaped, how many drowned we have no way of knowing.

4. **Continue along the B2075 to pass the lane to the farm with the confusingly similar name of Caldecott Farm. About 200 yards beyond the farm, and just before the B2075 meets the A259, a track turns off to the left. Turn left along the track.**

5. **The track follows a crooked course over the damp pasture land that is now Romney Marsh. Eventually it crosses a bridge and emerges on to a surfaced lane. Bear left at the lane, which runs south-west for about 250 yards before turning sharp left to cross a bridge.**

The walk bears off the B2075 along this farm track to wend its way over what is now damp, but rich pasture land but at the time of the battle was almost impassable swamp and marsh.

Near Point 5 on the walk this ruined medieval chapel can be seen across the fields. There is no direct access to the ruins which are, in any case, in an unsafe condition.

The level crossing that the walk passes between Points 5 and 6. Trains are not frequent, but care should still be taken at this little-used and ungated crossing.

This area has been carefully drained since the eighth century to produce sheep pasture, so it is much altered from its form when the battle took place. It remains a bleak, windswept place however. It was here that the Kentish fugitives sought to escape the Mercians. Some may have made it, many did not.

For Kent itself, however, there could be no escape. Praen was dragged off back to Lichfield where he had his hands cut off and his eyes put out. Cenwulf put his brother Cuthred on the throne of Kent to act as a puppet ruler while giving Kent the illusion of independence. When Cuthred died in 807 even the illusion was taken away. Kent became a province ruled directly by the Mercian king.

6. Continue along the lane to return to Lydd church.

6. CANTERBURY
851 & 1011

Distance:	1 mile.
Terrain:	City walk entirely over surfaced paths.
Public Transport:	Canterbury is served by main line railway and by numerous bus routes.
Parking:	Several off-street car parks in the city.
Refreshments:	Numerous pubs, cafés and restaurants in Canterbury, as well as shops that sell snacks and soft drinks.

Canterbury was an important town in pre-Roman times and became a local capital under Roman rule. It was the first city to pass to the Saxons, who were to become the English, and the only one to do so by treaty rather than conquest. Its later importance was due to the fact that it was here that St Augustine established his mission to convert the pagan English in 598.

In the year 602 St Augustine converted an existing church into a cathedral, making it the mother church of the English Christians. This original building was enlarged in the 750s but was still substantially standing in 851 when war came to the city. A short distance to the east, outside the city, St Augustine founded an abbey. In its early years the abbey rivalled the cathedral in importance. While the cathedral ministered to the spiritual needs of the lay community, the abbey held the theological library and acted as a centre for learning and erudition. Quite what form these buildings took in 851 we don't know, but it most likely had a small stone church acting as the focus for a variety of wooden monastic buildings.

Also standing in 851 were the Roman walls that surrounded the city. These were built mostly of stone, but with brick coursing at

△ The ruined nave of St Augustine's Abbey. Founded in 598, this was the oldest Catholic abbey in England but that did not save it from being closed down on the orders of King Henry VIII during the reformation.

▷ A statue of Queen Bertha, the first Christian queen of Kent, stands in public gardens in front of the entrance to Christ Church School as the walk approaches the old city walls.

The medieval gateway to the abbey is now incorporated into private buildings, the entrance blocked by a room, and is not open to the public.

intervals to help bind the stonework together. They stood around 20 feet tall and had bastions at intervals on which the Romans had mounted ballistae and other heavy machines able to throw stones or bolts considerable distances. Such sophisticated mechanical weapons had fallen out of use during the Dark Ages, and now the walls would be manned by local men armed with spears, backed up by a small professional core of soldiers with mail shirts, metal helmets and sidearms such as swords or knives as well as spears. English military equipment and tactics had not changed much since the battles at Lydd and Otford a generation or two earlier.

The men of Canterbury were going to need all the weapons they could muster, for marching against the city was a powerful force of Vikings, the largest yet known. The Viking raids had begun in 793 when the isolated island monastery of Lindisfarne in Northumberland was looted and destroyed, the monks being slain. As the years passed the Vikings came more and more often, and in greater numbers. In 840 a force of thirty-seven ships, each carrying around fifty men, attacked Southampton. Three years later 2,000 Vikings attacked Carhampton, but were driven off.

In 850 a vast army of some 15,000 Vikings was seen cruising up the Channel. They pillaged much of Devon, then climbed back in their ships and headed east, coasting off Kent until they reached Thanet, then still an island. There they landed, built a fortified base and settled down for the winter. The Vikings were clearly intending to pillage their way through England the following spring, and as the nearest city to Thanet Canterbury would be a prime target.

The Vikings came from the same military culture as the English, favouring the combination of shield and spear used in the shieldwall tactic. They did, however, introduce some innovations that did much to account for their success in battle. The first was the judicious use of their ships to flee from an unfavourable situation. At this period Viking armies tended to stay close to the beach or river where their ships were drawn up. If they found themselves facing a larger force, they would simply run off to get aboard their ships and go to search for easier victims.

Once battle was joined, the Vikings put into practice a variation on the shieldwall. Instead of forming up in a straight line, the wall was pushed forward at one or more places to form a 'hog's snout', or wedge shape. The best equipped and most experienced men were put into the 'hog's snout', which penetrated and broke up the enemy shieldwall as the two armies met.

One new weapon the Vikings brought with them was the ferocious Danish axe. This monstrous weapon was carried on a haft over 5 feet long and had a curved blade around 11 inches wide. In the hands of a skilled veteran, this axe could slice a man in half with ease. One record exists of such an axe cutting down through a man's helmet and skull to penetrate to the heart. It was a savage weapon and greatly feared, though the fact that it had to be used two-handed meant that the wielder could not carry a shield into battle.

Since the Battle of Lydd, Kent had been part of Mercia so it fell to King Brihtwulf of Mercia to defend the city and surrounding country. The problem was that the Vikings might clamber into their ships to attack almost anywhere along the eastern coast of England. Rather than mass his men in Kent, Brihtwulf seems to have ordered his army to muster at London as the spring weather heralded the coming of the campaigning season. He would then have waited to see where the Vikings went before marching to meet them.

As things turned out, the Viking army took the obvious course and marched on Canterbury. The local men manned the walls, and sent hurried messages off to London to summon the royal army to their aid.

Walk 6. Canterbury

THE WALK

1. In Canterbury find St Augustine's Abbey, which lies just east of the city centre. It is well signposted from all approach roads.

Standing outside the city walls as it did, St Augustine's Abbey was the first target for the advancing Viking horde. The monks had already retreated behind the city walls, carrying with them their

The round late-medieval towers north of Bur Gate were erected when an invasion from France seemed likely. They were not here at the time of the Viking siege, though the wall was of about the present height and thickness.

Canterbury Cathedral floats above the houses of the city, seen from Burgate. The present building is medieval in date, but stands on the site of the old English minster that was here when the Vikings attacked.

precious books and religious relics, but the buildings soon fell victim. They were looted thoroughly of anything useful, then torched. Nothing remains of that first monastery, so thorough were the Vikings in their work of destruction. The ruins to be seen today date largely from the thirteenth century.

2. Leave the ruins, walking west along Longport, turning north up Monastery Street and then turning left into Lady Wooton's Green. This short road ends in a T-junction with Lower Bridge Street on the far side of which stands a remaining section of Canterbury's city walls.

The walls to be seen today date largely from the thirteenth century, but the lower sections and foundations are of Roman and English date, so these would have been here in 851 to face the Vikings. Ferocious and skilled at battle, the Vikings may have been but they came from a land without stone walls and had no experience at all in assaulting cities or fortifications of brick and stone. They may have attempted to fire the wooden gates or even to scale the walls with ladders. Perhaps more likely the Vikings fanned out over the surrounding countryside to steal whatever had not been carried into the city for safety.

After some days the watching defenders on these walls saw a sudden stir in the Viking camp. The heathen raiders formed up and marched off to the west. Unknown to the Canterbury men, King Brihtwulf was marching to their rescue with the royal army of Mercia.

A few days later the Vikings were back, carrying with them the spoils of victory. We do not know where the battle between Brihtwulf and the Vikings took place, except that it was somewhere between London and Canterbury. The Mercians came off worse and retreated back to London. The Viking victory was not

△ Left: The Butter Market, the small square at the western end of Burgate is marked by this cross. The entrance to the cathedral close stands on the northern side of the square. Right: The modern statue of Christ that stands over the gateway that gives access to the cathedral close.

▽ Parade Street is one of the major shopping streets in Canterbury, as it has been since the city was redeveloped by the Romans in about AD 49.

complete for Brihtwulf escaped alive and his army was largely intact. Canterbury, however, was abandoned to its fate.

There is no record of any damage inside the city walls in 851, so it must be presumed that the Vikings were bought off with a payment of cash. Gathering their booty, the Vikings set off up the Thames to investigate the possibilities of rape and pillage further to the west. They came to grief at the hands of King Athelwulf of Wessex and that autumn the survivors streamed back down the Thames.

3. Turn left along Lower Bridge Street, keeping the city walls on your right. After about 200 yards there is a break in the city walls at Bur Gate. The actual gate itself was demolished two centuries ago, but the modern road of Burgate which runs into the city centre shows where it once stood.

In 1009 the Vikings returned to Canterbury. This time we know the name of their leader, Thorkell the Tall, a Danish noble-man. By this date the Vikings had become rather more adept at siege warfare, learning how to make and use battering rams and other machines of war. However, Thorkell was in a hurry to get on to the richer pickings of the Midlands. He demanded and got 3,000 pounds of silver coin in return for leaving the city and county alone, then moved on.

Two years later Thorkell and his men were back. The Vikings had spent the time running rings around the English King Ethelred the Unready. They had plundered their way across sixteen counties, defeated one English army and eluded two others. Now they were on their way home, and perhaps Thorkell thought to squeeze some more ready cash out of Kent before he left.

In the event Thorkell and his Vikings achieved far more than mere extortion. Inside Canterbury was a man named Almaer who

A Viking warrior. He carries a pair of throwing javelins as well as an axe and shield. Like most Viking warriors he comes to battle equipped with a mail shirt and metal helmet that would have been worn by only the richer Englishmen.

was as treacherous as he was greedy. In return for a cash prize, he opened one of the eastern gates to the Vikings at the dead of night. Which gate he opened is not certain, but it may well have been the Bur Gate.

4. Turn right through the site of the Bur Gate and walk west along Burgate. Where the street opens out into a small square a large gatehouse dominates the scene on the right. This is the entrance to the cathedral close. There is an entrance fee to pay to enter the close and the cathedral. The beautiful buildings within are well worth the price, but you need not enter if you choose not to as the walk passes back out of this gate.

The Vikings surged up Burgate, battered down the wooden gates that stood there in those days and poured into the cathedral close. The cathedral that they found in front of them was the late Roman stone church that had been taken over by St Augustine three centuries earlier. They wasted little time in ransacking their way through the surrounding timber and brick buildings. They quickly seized Archbishop Alfheah and Abbot Leofwine, but other clerics fled to the cathedral and barricaded the doors shut. The Vikings promptly set fire to the church, and only four monks managed to escape alive.

Meanwhile the sacking of the city proceeded thoroughly and in determined fashion. The usual excesses of rape and pillage took place in the days that followed. Then the Vikings settled down to stay in Canterbury for some weeks while they waited for news of the ransom that they were demanding for the safe release of the Archbishop.

Of the ecclesiastical buildings that the Vikings found here in 1011, no trace remains above ground. The cathedral was rebuilt after the Vikings left, then again in 1070 after a second fire reduced the new building to ashes. Of this third church the crypt remains intact, as does some work above ground, but most of the current building dates from later centuries.

After kicking their heels in Canterbury for some weeks, the Vikings grew bored with waiting for the money to arrive. They decided to leave the city for a place where they could beach their ships and camp beside them within a hastily built wooden enclosure.

5. Leave the cathedral precincts and cross the small square to head south-west along Mercer's Lane.

6. This short road ends at a junction with High Street running to the right and Parade Street to the left. Turn left along Parade Street. This road runs along the route of the main thoroughfare of Roman Canterbury and was one of the widest streets in the city at the time of the Viking occupation. Viking warriors marched down this street on their way out of

The charming cottages of Love Lane, some of which are over 400 years old. These were among the first houses to spread outside the city walls as England became a peaceful kingdom.

the ruined city. Follow the street to pass out of the city walls once again.

When they left Canterbury, the Vikings marched off to Greenwich. There they built their fortified camp and settled down for the winter. The ransom negotiations for the unfortunate archbishop had stipulated that 8,000 pounds of silver had to be paid by Easter Sunday, 13 April. On the Saturday English envoys arrived to make arrangements for the payments. As they were talking to Thorkell the Tall, Archbishop Alfheah broke free and ran towards the envoys. He told them in no uncertain terms that no ransom was to be paid for him, a mere humble servant of Christ, to such brutal pagan raiders. Startled, the envoys rode off.

That night the Vikings held a great feast at which they roasted several whole oxen and drank prodigious quantities of plundered wine. One group of Vikings grabbed Alfheah and dragged him to a post set up beside the cooking fire. They then began to throw bones and rubbish at the cleric. Thorkell the Tall tried to intervene, but was shouted down and pushed roughly aside by his own men. The attacks on the archbishop became rougher and more drunken as he was pelted with ox bones and even a severed ox head until he collapsed on the ground and was finished off with an axe.

The Vikings left a few days later, leaving the murdered archbishop's body lying where it had fallen. Canterbury Cathedral was a smoke-blackened wreck so the body was taken to St Paul's Cathedral in London for burial. Thorkell had been so shocked by what happened that while the majority of his army sailed home over the North Sea, he stayed in England and offered his services, and those of his men who chose to stay with him, to the English king.

6. Cross over the main road junction, using the pedestrian underpass to avoid the busy traffic. You may then use the footpath that runs into Love Lane to return to the start of the walk. Alternatively, head east along St George's Place and after about 150 yards, turn left into Lower Chantry Lane and follow this road back to the abbey.

7. HASTINGS
1066

Distance:	3¾ miles
Terrain:	This walk is partly over unsurfaced footpaths, though most are in good condition. There are two hills, neither of which is especially steep.
Public Transport:	The walk starts and finishes at Battle railway station.
Parking:	A few parking spaces at the station and several off-street car parks in the town.
Refreshments:	Several pubs and restaurants in Battle, as well as shops that sell snacks and soft drinks.

In January 1066 King Edward the Confessor of England lay dying. He had no children, a fact that would plunge his kingdom into war and change the face of England, and of Britain, forever.

It was not that there was a shortage of potential heirs – the difficulty was that there were too many and none had a claim to the throne that was any better than the others. It was up to the Witan, the council of nobles, to decide who should be the next king. Tradition demanded that they should choose a member of the royal family, but beyond that they were free to choose who they liked. In terms of strict legitimacy the crown should have passed to Edgar the Atheling, great nephew of Edward the Confessor. However Edgar was a mere child who had been brought up in Hungary and few people supported his cause.

Next to be considered was Harold Godwinson, Earl of Wessex and head of the powerful Godwinson family. Harold had only a tenuous link to the crown. He was a member of the royal family by marriage, his sister being Edward's queen. Unlike Edgar, Harold was a grown man of forty-four with a proven track record of mili-

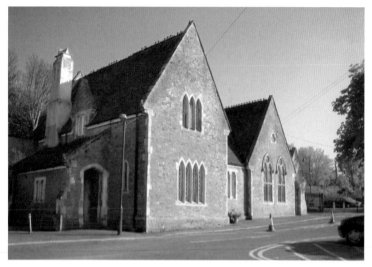

Battle railway station, where the walk begins and ends, stands on what was the reverse slope of the English position behind the left flank of Harold's line.

At the end of the track opposite the station, the walk climbs over this stile to enter a field and pass along what was the front of the initial Norman position on the day of battle.

tary success against the Welsh and of administrative skill in his earldom. He had, moreover, travelled on pilgrimage to Rome and had contacts abroad.

Also related to the royal family by marriage, though more distantly, was Duke William of Normandy. His great aunt Emma had married Ethelred the Unready and so was mother to Edward the Confessor. What William did have, or so he claimed, was a promise from Edward to nominate him as successor should he die without a son. The promise appears to have been made in 1051 during some complex diplomatic moves between England and Normandy. If any of the nobles in England were aware of the promise they showed no signs of taking it very seriously.

A fourth contender lurked across the North Sea in the shape of King Harald Hardrada of Norway. Hardrada had no real claim to the throne at all, but he had friends and supporters in England. Moreover he was a big, tough and confident ruler who could command a mighty army of Vikings.

For the English noblemen meeting at Westminster as Edward lay dying the decision seemed an easy one. Harold Godwinson was English and he was capable. If any of them had any doubts, these were quelled when Edward indicated that Harold should be the next king. Edward died on 5 January and was buried next day. As soon as Edward was laid in his grave the nobles proclaimed Harold king and he was crowned later the same day.

Harold was under no illusions. He learned early in the summer that William of Normandy was gathering an army and fleet with which to invade England. The English army was mustered in Kent, but when September arrived with no sign of William Harold disbanded the army. It was at this point that he heard that Hardrada had landed in Yorkshire.

Hurriedly Harold raced north with his huscarls, his personal troops, gathering forces as he marched. The Vikings had defeated the local levies on 19 September and were lazing about awaiting envoys from York bringing tribute when Harold and his army appeared. The subsequent Battle of Stamford Bridge was an overwhelming victory for Harold, but he lost a good number of men in the fighting.

Four days after the defeat of Hardrada, William of Normandy landed at Pevensey in Sussex. Harold at once sent riders racing south ordering the men of the southern shires to muster at London. He then led his army south, arriving in London just six days after leaving York. Five days later he was on the march again, this time heading south to face the army of Duke William, which was now camped around Hastings.

Harold left orders that any troops not yet arrived should march to 'the hoar apple tree', which stood on a hill some distance north of Hastings. He reached the spot on the afternoon of 13 October.

The English army that Harold led to the hoar apple tree was exclusively infantry in make up, though many men would have ridden to battle. In equipment and tactics, the English by 1066 were a blend of the earlier English and Viking armies that had fought at Canterbury, Lydd and Otford. Most men had rudimentary armour of toughened leather, while a few had mail shirts and metal helmets. Nearly all men carried shield and spear, with an axe or short sword as a secondary weapon. A few men carried the terrifying double-handed axe introduced by the Vikings. This weapon would come as a rude shock to the Normans in the battle that followed.

A key innovation by 1066 was in the organisation of the army. While the majority were farmers and workmen serving as part-time soldiers with only basic training in holding a shieldwall formation, the English now had huscarls. These professional soldiers were permanently attached to the king and earls that they served. They wore the finest armour and carried the best weapons available, and they trained full time in the arts of war. It was these huscarls that clustered around their lord and formed the front rank of an army in battle.

It seems that Harold intended to rest around the hoar apple tree on 14 October while his army arrived and was organised for battle. He would then advance to attack Hastings where William had constructed temporary wood and earthen fortifications. But about three hours after dawn Harold's scouts on Telham Hill spotted the Norman army advancing up the road from Hastings.

Harold quickly arranged his army for battle. The huscarls formed up in the centre around the royal banner and formed up as a front rank along the crest of the hill. Behind them came the mass of the English army. Harold's plan seems to have been to stand on the defensive behind the shieldwall and allow William to slog up the hill and batter against the wall. Once the Normans had lost enough men, the English would advance down the hill to win the victory.

Harold may have had some 7,000 men with him at dawn, with as many as 4,000 others on their way in small and scattered units.

Harold had good reason to wait on the defensive. Not only was his army still arriving, but William had brought with him a formidable new weapon. Harold had seen it in action and knew it could be horribly effective. William had brought mounted, armoured knights.

These knights were to dominate the battlefields of Europe for centuries to come. Each man wore mail armour that reached from the top of his head down to his wrists and knees. He carried a large, kite-shaped shield that protected his entire left side in battle and wore a helmet that added to the protection of the mail over his head. Thus protected, the knights were almost immune to most weapons of the time. A sword or spear would have trouble cutting through the mail, though a really heavy blow could break

A Norman knight. He wears a mail shirt to his knees and has a metal helmet. His long shield would protect his leg and the horse's flank. The lance could be used crouched or overam for thrusting and his sword was used for close-quarter combat.

the bones beneath the armour and so put the knight out of the fight.

The preferred tactic of the Normans was to form up their knights into a compact body some three ranks deep and riding stirrup to stirrup. They would then advance at the trot, breaking into a gallop as they approached the enemy. The momentum built up by the charging horsemen was often enough to burst through an enemy formation, and sometimes the mere sight of the charging knights would cause an enemy to flee. Once the enemy formation was disrupted, the knights would use lances and swords to hack at the enemy, turning defeat into rout and inflicting heavy casualties.

William probably had about 3,000 knights with him, plus another 6,000 or so infantry. His army outnumbered the English on the hill at dawn, but would be outnumbered in turn when the entire English army arrived.

Just as Harold knew he had to keep his shieldwall intact until the horsemen were exhausted, William knew he had to smash the formation early if he was to win. William had therefore brought with him substantial numbers of archers and infantry whose job was to attack first to wear down the English and render them vulnerable to a mounted charge.

As the English scouts fell back and the Norman army appeared over the crest of Telham Hill it was clear that the battle was about to begin. Soon Harold and William would know whose battle plan was going to win.

THE WALK

1. Leave Battle railway station, walking south-west along the access road, Station Approach. This reaches a T-junction with the main A2100, a busy road that needs to be crossed with care. Cross this main road and turn left. After barely 50 yards turn right into a narrow close that ends after about 150 yards. A footpath continues straight ahead over a stile and into open fields. At the end of the wood on the right pause to look up the slope to your left.

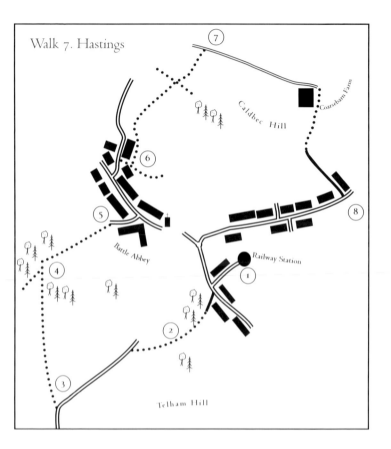

Walk 7. Hastings

This hill is Telham Hill, over the crest of which William's army appeared at about 8am. The old road from London to Hastings ran slightly to the south of the modern A2100 and probably passed over these fields. As the English scouts rode back to Harold, William led his army down this slope to form up in the valley bottom. The centre of the Norman army formed up at more or less the spot where you are now standing.

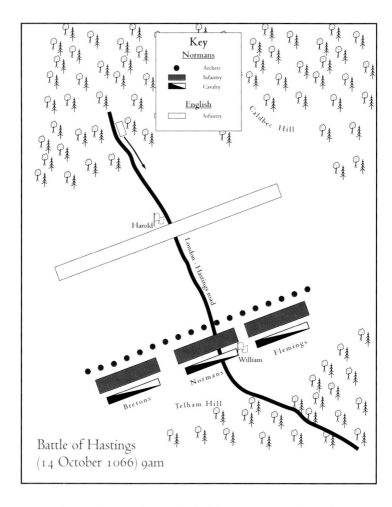

Battle of Hastings
(14 October 1066) 9am

We know that William divided his army into three divisions, based on the nationality of the men. The Normans were in the centre, commanded by William himself. On the left was a division made up of Bretons who had been recruited by William with lavish

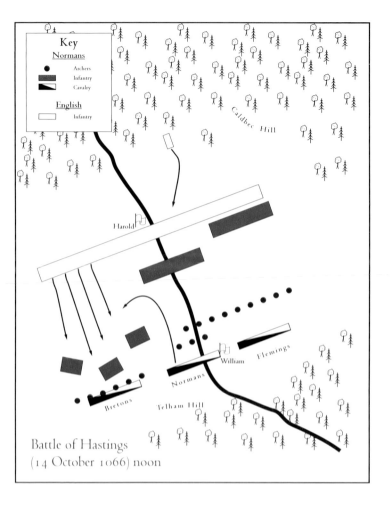

Battle of Hastings
(14 October 1066) noon

promises of loot to be had in England. The right was taken up by
a mixed body of French and Flemings, likewise hired by William.

Each division was organised in similar fashion. In the front rank
were archers, in open formation. Behind them came a compact

The view up the hill from the valley floor toward what was the right flank of the English position. The woods to the right of this picture form the grounds of Battle Abbey. The lone tree on the horizon marks the hill summit where the English army drew up.

The walk from the signpost to the abbey goes along this surfaced track at the summit of the hill. Harold drew up his men in a shieldwall formation facing south along this line.

body of infantry equipped with shields, spears and swords. Behind them stood the mounted knights awaiting the order to charge. It is likely that the Norman army was formed up on the lower slopes of Telham Hill, so the modern path probably runs along the front of the loosely organised archers.

Turn now to look across the valley and up to the hill to the north. This was where the English formed up. We know precisely where Harold erected the English royal banner because the high altar of Battle Abbey was put on the spot after the battle. The church has now been demolished, but it stood just to the right of the cluster of buildings that still stand. The whole of the ridge, stretching about 800 yards and centred on the banner, was filled with the English army. They formed a single, solid shieldwall from behind which the English chanted and sang their confidence in victory.

It must have been a daunting sight for the Normans and their allies forming up here in the valley. Seeing that the men were eyeing the English army with apprehension William's personal minstrel, Taillefer, spurred his horse up the slope to the English line. He then gambolled about performing riding tricks that are today seen in circuses and juggling with his sword while all the time singing songs in praise of Duke William. The Normans cheered. The English jeered. Then an English warrior stepped forward from the shieldwall and with a single thrust of his spear killed Taillefer.

2. Continue along the footpath until it emerges on to a road. Turn left on the road, taking care as there is no footpath for the first few yards. Continue along what was the front of the Norman army as it formed up. Where the road turns sharp left, a farm track continues straight on. Take this drive, then almost immediately turn right over a stile and along a foot-path. Walk downhill along a gravel track. At the end of this

track use a gate to pick up a footpath that runs over grass to a second gate. This gives access to a narrow path between two fences, at the end of which a further gate opens on to a grassy field which sweeps uphill.

This path follows the route taken by the Flemings in their attack on the right wing of the English army. William gave the order to attack at about 9.30am. First into action were the crossbowmen, archers in other sections of the Norman line, who got to about 100 yards from the English line before halting and beginning to shoot. For some minutes the missiles were sent flying toward the English line. Few, if any, arrows came in reply for the English had very few archers on the field and they were conserving their arrows for when the real action began. After a few minutes shooting, the crossbowmen were down to their last few bolts and stopped shooting.

Now the infantry advanced up the slope. They no doubt began the advance in a form of shieldwall, but the broken nature of the ground and the fairly steep slope caused the formation to loosen up slightly. By the time the Bretons reached the English line on the ridge above their formation had some dangerous gaps in it. The English huscarls in the front rank were highly skilled fighters who knew how to exploit a disordered enemy.

After a period of intense hand-to-hand combat, the Bretons broke and fell back down the hill. As they pulled back their formation became even more disordered until the Breton infantry were little more than a fleeing mob. Seeing them go, the Norman infantry in the centre began to fall back, albeit in more orderly formation. In turn the Flemings on the right likewise broke off their attack.

As the enemy fell back, the English were jubilant. Those on the right of the line thought that the moment had come for the planned counterattack and surged down the hill to cut down the fleeing Bretons. At the foot of the hill, where the stream runs, the Breton infantry collided with their rear rank of knights, throwing them into confusion. Into this disorganised mass plunged the English.

At some point a Breton knight went down. A cry went up that Duke William had been killed. The Norman infantry looked around in confusion and pulled back even faster, their formation beginning to collapse as they tried to march backward over broken ground with too much haste. At this moment, William spurred forward from his position at the head of the Norman knights. He removed his helmet and bellowed at the Norman infantry to look at him, recognise him and stand firm.

It was the crisis of the battle for William. Fortunately for him his men recognised him and rallied. As the Norman infantry reformed, William could turn his attention to the disaster unfolding on his left among the Bretons. The English were doing fearful havoc to the Bretons, and the Breton knights were almost helpless as their horses got stuck down in the boggy ground around the stream. William led his Norman knights in a charge that wheeled to their left and slammed into the flank and rear of the English. Attacking disordered infantry, the knights were unstoppable. Very few English managed to get back to their ridge alive.

It was now noon and a pause followed while both commanders reformed their troops. At around 2pm William launched a new attack. This time he sent in his mounted knights to smash the English line in a co-ordinated and compact charge. But the English shieldwall was still intact, so the Norman knights would have to break it before they could wreak havoc.

3. Walk up the hill to reach the crest of the ridge. This is the place where the Norman cavalry crashed into the English shieldwall.

Harold was not content to rely merely on his shieldwall. At intervals he had placed huscarls armed with the ferocious double-handed axes standing just in advance of the line where they had room to make the necessary mighty swinging movements. Now the Normans met this weapon for the first time and were appalled by its savage effectiveness. A single blow could decapitate a horse, slice a man in half – even through armour – or kill horse and rider in a single sweeping arc of death.

The initial charge inflicted casualties, but did not break the English shieldwall. Again and again the Normans charged, again and again they were thrown back. William was getting desperate.

He now carried out a feigned retreat. He ordered one group of knights to pull back, tempting the English in that section of the line to attack, and then swung a second group of knights in to attack them on the flank. The trick worked and many English were killed, but it would not work again.

It was now almost 4pm and the light was beginning to fade as the autumn afternoon drew to a close. William now changed his tactics. He brought the archers forward again and ordered them to use their few remaining arrows to aim high so that their arrows fell down on the rear ranks of the English rather that striking the shields and armour of the huscarls in the front rank. Meanwhile the infantry and knights were brought forward and told to attack any weak spots that they saw.

The first weak point appeared here, on the English right flank. Taking their chance, the knights charged and this time they broke through the shieldwall. The fighting was savage, but the English line had been broken. The right flank collapsed as the men streamed away northward seeking the safety of the forest beyond the ridge.

△ The great gatehouse to Battle Abbey. The Abbey was founded by William after the battle with the high altar being placed on the spot where Harold's banner stood during the fighting.

▷ The entrance to the Battle Abbey is marked by this signpost. The grounds of the abbey can be visited on the course of the walk if wished.

Battle of Hastings 1066
Abbey and Historic Battlefield

Site of King Harold's defeat by William the Conqueror

Exhibition: History from 1066 to 1600

Introductory video and inclusive audio tour

New Exhibition: Prelude to Battle

Children's play area   Gift shop   Picnic area

4. At the summit of the ridge, bear right keeping the fence that marks the boundary of Battle Abbey grounds on your right. The path meets another beside a wooden finger post. Turn right, following the edge of a fenced wood. This path ends at a surfaced lane. Continue straight on along the lane to pass a car park on the right. After 150 yards the imposing bulk of Battle Abbey gatehouse appears on the right. You are now standing behind the centre of the English army. The abbey charges for admittance, but its grounds do contain the position of the English centre and a plaque marks the spot where King Harold stood at this vital moment in the battle. If you choose to enter the abbey, make your way to this plaque which is to be found inside the ruined abbey church. If not, pause here then continue the walk as the route comes back out of the abbey gatehouse.

As the right wing of the English army collapsed, so did the left wing. In the centre Harold had already been wounded, traditionally by an arrow that struck his eye. Around him huscarls were fighting to hold their section of shieldwall against the Norman attacks. As the light began to fade the slaughter in this area was frightful. Even the Norman chroniclers remarked on it.

Then four knights burst through the shieldwall and reached the wounded Harold. They cut him down, one man hacking off his leg with a sword. Still the huscarls fought on for it was a matter of pride and honour that they must never leave their lord.

By now it was around 5.30pm. As Harold died the English army broke up and fled. The Normans set off in pursuit.

5. Leave the gatehouse and turn left to walk north-west up Battle High Street. After about 200 yards, turn right into Caldbec Hill Lane. Ignore the turning to the car park, but take

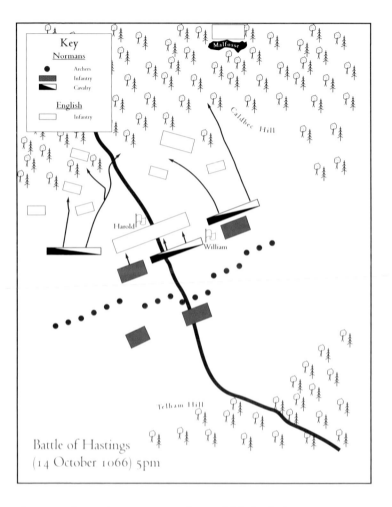

Battle of Hastings
(14 October 1066) 5pm

the second turn into a narrow lane which leads between some
houses. Beyond the garages on the left turn left into a footpath
that runs across open fields up Caldbec Hill itself. At the
summit of the hill the path meets a surfaced drive. Turn right.

At the time of the battle this hill was wooded, as was most of the country hereabouts. Somewhere in this area the Norman pursuit came to a sudden and bloody end. A large group of knights were galloping forward in the gathering dusk when they ran into a group of advancing English troops who had not been involved in the fighting. The knights were taken by surprise, especially as their horses fell headlong into a ditch that they had not seen in the gloom. Dozens were killed. The pursuit was called off and the battle was over. This ditch was dubbed Malfosse – meaning 'evil ditch' by the Normans.

7. Continue along the lane until it crosses over the railway line and ends at Coarsebarn Farm. A path then strikes south over the fields and down the hill. After 200 yards the path becomes a surfaced track beside a water treatment works. This bends to the left and runs beside a housing estate to emerge on to Marley Lane.

8. Turn right along Marley Lane to enter the town of Battle. Go over a level crossing. Where the lane meets a small roundabout, turn left and return to the railway station.

With Harold dead, English resistance to William became disorganised. Some nobles and cities declared for Edgar, others opened their gates to the Normans. London held out for some weeks, but it eventually became clear that most of England's fighting strength had been destroyed at Stamford Bridge and Hastings. William was accepted as king and crowned in December.

No doubt many English hoped the conquest meant merely a new king, but they soon learned that it entailed so much more. William exterminated or dispossessed nearly every English nobleman, even English clerics lost their positions in the Church. The

The surfaced track along the top of Telham Hill looking east. The notorious Malfosse lay somewhere just off this lane, but the exact location has been lost.

old system of land holding, government and administration was swept away to be replaced by Norman-style feudalism. It would be two centuries before English again became the language of the nobility and of government. Meanwhile, England was ruled by foreigners who often cared more for their lands in Normandy and France than for England.

8. ROCHESTER
1215, 1264 & 1667

Distance:	1 mile.
Terrain:	City walk entirely over surfaced paths.
Public Transport:	The walk starts and finishes at the railway station.
Parking:	Several off-street car parks in the city.
Refreshments:	Numerous pubs, cafes and restaurants in Rochester, as well as shops that sell snacks and soft drinks.

As the lowest crossing point over the River Medway, Rochester has long had a strategic importance to both merchants and the military. The pre-Roman Cantium tribe had a settlement here and may just possibly have built a timber bridge where the Romans later erected a stone bridge, just upstream of the modern bridge. That bridge for centuries carried the main Dover to London road.

As a prosperous town astride a strategic river, Rochester was twice attacked by the Vikings. In 884 the city was besieged by a large army of Danish Vikings, but held out for six months before King Alfred the Great arrived with his army, at which point the Vikings fled. Another army from across the North Sea arrived in 999 and this time captured the town. We have no reliable accounts of those attacks, so it is impossible to work out how they developed on the ground.

It was here that William the Conqueror decided to build one of the most powerful castles in England soon after he conquered the country in 1066. When William died in 1087 the throne was disputed between his eldest son Robert, to whom William had left Normandy, and the younger son William Rufus, who had been left England by his father. Robert's supporters included his uncle Bishop Odo of Bayeux, who owned Rochester at the time. William Rufus moved swiftly to put the rebellion down, capturing Rochester after a

The sole surviving section of Rochester's medieval town walls, themselves built on the foundations of the Roman walls that preceded them. The skirmish that began the siege of 1215 took place on the flat land just outside these walls to the right of the photo.

siege of six weeks. Again no details of the fighting survive.

It was William Rufus's brother and successor Henry I who built the castle that we see today. The massive central keep stands on a base 70 feet square and is over 110 feet tall. The walls are 14 feet thick and built of solid stone, which made them impenetrable to any siege engines of the time. Rochester Castle had a reputation for being impervious to assault.

The city that stood beside the castle was likewise fortified, though the city walls could not match those of the castle either for height or thickness. Rochester has been the seat of a bishopric since the early seventh century, making this the second oldest in England after Canterbury. The cathedral stands close to the castle and dates

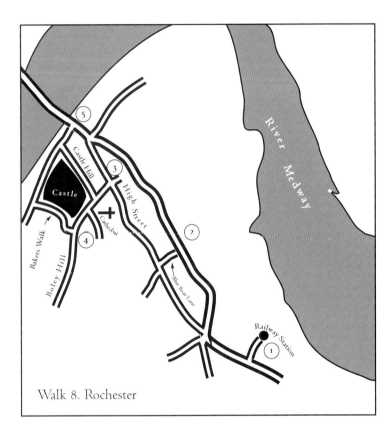

Walk 8. Rochester

largely from the twelfth century, so like the castle it stood here during the great siege of 1215.

The year 1215 is most famous as being the year in which King John signed the Magna Carta which, among various other important provisions, established that even the king had to obey the law, and that nobody could be imprisoned without fair trial – the latter principle being generally termed *habeas corpus*. What is not generally known, however, is that one group of barons wanted to go further by subject-

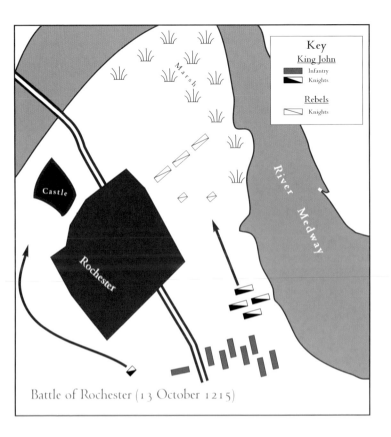

Battle of Rochester (13 October 1215)

ing the king to baronial supervision. When John refused to agree to this war broke out between the more radical barons and the king.

The barons were led by Robert FitzWalter and William Albini, Count Aumale. John caught them by surprise, leading his armies rapidly around England reinforcing castle garrisons loyal to the king and seizing lands belonging to the rebels. But John was short of men. Once the rebels got their act together they would probably have the greater force and John knew it. Having bolstered his

△   Left: Rochester High Street. This street echoed to the sounds of armoured footsteps as King John's men chased the baronial forces through the town after the skirmish outside the walls. Right: The College Gate. It was this gate that led through the town walls from the town to the castle. The upper storey is more recent having been erected as a comfortable lodging after the walls were no longer needed for defence.

▽   Rochester Cathedral, almost unaltered from how it appeared in 1215. At the time of the siege the town walls ran immediately in front of the cathedral's west end, where the road in the photograph now runs.

defences, John moved to Dover and sent messages overseas hiring mercenaries to come and support his cause.

While John was holed up in Dover, FitzWalter sent out messages mustering the rebels in London, while Albini hurried to Rochester. Commanding the road from Dover to London the city and castle were a key strategic communications centre for the coming campaign. In the last week of September Albini entered Rochester with 140 knights and their retinues, perhaps 400 men in all. On 7 October he was joined by FitzWalter and the entire force that had so far rallied to the rebel cause, about 500 knights, who camped on the flat meadows between Rochester and the river.

On 11 October King John set out from Dover with a small force of English knights and footsoldiers, plus a considerable army of mercenaries. Two nights later the royal army camped outside Gillingham and on the morning of 13 October King John hoisted the royal banner and began the short march to Rochester. The great siege of Rochester was about to begin.

After the dramatic events of 1215, Rochester would be besieged once more, in 1264. It would see battle once more, with the events of 1667, which rank among the most astonishing and ignominious in the history Britain's Royal Navy.

THE WALK

1. Leave Rochester railway station and turn right to walk east along the High Street for 100 yards before turning right again to follow the A2 inner ring road. This road runs to the east of the old town through a Victorian area that is currently undergoing much redevelopment. Pause where Blue Boar Lane turns left beside traffic lights. A section of the old city walls is visible in front of you and to your left.

◁ The mighty keep of Rochester Castle. In 1215 this was considered to be one of the finest castles in Europe and to be effectively impregnable, though King John was determined to capture it.

▽ The bridge over the Medway at Rochester. The construction is modern, but it gives a good idea of the width of the river at this point. The medieval bridge was carried on about fifteen piers.

The area to your right is now dominated by the railway viaduct and assorted industrial buildings. In 1215, however, this was open land between Rochester city walls and the marshes that bordered the Medway. The damp meadows were often flooded in winter, but that October they were dry and firm.

The rebels saw the royal banners advancing about mid-morning and stood to arms. Albini's men lined the walls of the city and castle, while FitzWalter's mounted knights formed up in several groups on the meadows. There they blocked the route around Rochester to the all important bridge beyond.

King John was an experienced and able soldier, though one who preferred the luxuries of peace to the rigours of campaign. This day, however, he was most certainly on campaign and determined to defeat the rebels. He led his forces up to Rochester. While he stationed his infantry in the rear with orders to adopt a defensive formation behind interlocked shields, he sent his herald to the gates of the city to demand instant surrender.

When the royal herald approached the gates under the royal banner, a sudden panic struck the citizens who had climbed up to the walls to watch the coming battle. They fled, their panic spreading rapidly through the city. Suddenly hundreds of men, women and children were scrambling into carts, loading down pack horses with anything of value and streaming out of the city's West Gate to pour over the bridge. Albini's men got swept along with the move. They abandoned the walls and fled toward the castle.

Seeing the walls suddenly emptying of men, King John gave the order to attack the rebel knights in the meadows. FitzWalter and his men had also seen the sudden movement on the walls of Rochester. FitzWalter sent some of his knights forward in small bodies to challenge the advancing royal forces. There were skirmishes and struggles as the leading knights on both sides clashed. The rebel outriders were pushed back, one of them being unhorsed and captured.

Drawing back his forward units, King John began drawing up his knights into a compact body to deliver a concentrated charge at the rebels. FitzWalter saw that his knights were beginning to waver. Rather than face the awesome power of a charge by mounted, armoured knights, FitzWalter turned and led his men north-west to cross the bridge and head for London. He sent one man to the castle with a hurried message to Albini. FitzWalter promised to return as soon as the main rebel force had reached London. And then he was gone.

2. Turn left up Blue Boar Lane to where it joins the High Street. Turn right.

It was down this street that Albini's men fled to reach the castle. As FitzWalter's men raced over the bridge, those citizens of Rochester who were loyal to the king opened the gates to him and his forces. It was now early afternoon. Again armed and armoured men pounded down this street, but this time it was men loyal to King John seeking to get into the castle before the rebels could secure it. They were too late. The gates were shut fast.

3. Where the High Street meets Boley Hill at a crossroads the castle comes into view to the left. Turn left. Pass the cathedral on your left and face the castle.

In 1215 the city walls ran along the line of Boley Hill. The cathedral faced the castle through a gate. It was at this gate that perhaps the most astonishing incident of the entire siege took place. The knight unhorsed and captured in the meadows was Sir Oliver Argentan. He was the younger son of a not particularly wealthy family from the Midlands whose father had spent the family assets training and equipping his son as a knight. There was no money left in the family coffers to afford a ransom and so his life was forfeit as a rebel.

King John had the hapless Sir Oliver brought up to the battlements here to be hanged as an example to the rebel garrison in the castle. As Sir Oliver was led out, a sudden shout went up from the castle. On the walls was Sir Oliver's older brother Sir Richard Argentan. Sir Richard did not have enough money to pay the ransom either, but he did shout across to King John a unique proposal. If the king would spare the life of his younger brother, Sir Richard said he would change sides and fight on the side of the king. John was clearly surprised, but he could see the value of the deal. Young Sir William was set free and given a horse on which to ride home, while Sir Richard slipped out of the gates, opened for a moment to allow the move, and crossed over to the king's side. He served King John loyally until the king's death.

Meanwhile, the siege was proceeding. Although Rochester Castle was widely rumoured to be impregnable, King John was determined to capture the place as quickly as possible. Among the mercenaries he had hired was a gang of German miners skilled in digging underground passages. These men were put to work inside a house beside Rochester Cathedral. First they tore up the floor, then dug straight down about 20 feet before starting to tunnel toward the castle walls.

To disguise the tunnelling from the defenders, John insisted that a regular siege be undertaken. Catapults and other siege engines were constructed and began to batter at the walls. Archers and crossbowmen were installed on the city walls to shoot at the castle battlements to try to pick off the defenders. Albini, of course, had his own archers and crossbowmen and ordered them to shoot back at the attackers. On one occasion, King John came forward to supervise and rode within crossbow range. One of the castle's crossbowmen put his bolt in his weapon and eagerly drew aim at the king. Albini knocked the weapon from his hands. 'It is not for us to kill the Lord's anointed,' he declared.

At the end of October, John ordered his men to attack the outer bailey, visible to the right as you look at the castle from the cathedral, by storm. A deluge of bolts and arrows swept the battlements as men stormed forward to clamber up on ladders. The assault was a success and the bailey fell. But still the mighty keep held out.

On 25 November the German miners reported that they were at last under the keep and ready. The wooden props holding up the roof of the tunnel were smeared with pig's fat and packed around with straw and twigs. Then the whole lot was set on fire. As the wooden props burned through they collapsed, bringing down the tunnel roof above and so one entire corner of the keep fell with a deafening crash. John's men swarmed up the mound of rubble, but Albini recovered from the shock quickly and ordered all interior doors to be bolted and barricaded. By nightfall John's men had captured half the keep, but failed to penetrate the rest.

For five days the two forces battled each other in the shattered wreck of the keep. Finally, on 30 November King John offered terms. He offered to spare the lives of all within and to set reasonable ransoms for the release of all. John made only one exception: the crossbowman who had tried to shoot him. Albini agreed and surrendered. The hapless crossbowman was hanged immediately.

The capture of Rochester Castle restored John's fortunes and revived his cause. Many nobles who had remained neutral now joined the king, while others who had been riding to join the rebels went home. Even so FitzWalter had powerful forces at his back. The war dragged on until John died the following year. With John dead and the elderly and much respected Earl William Marshal acting as regent for the infant King Henry III the rebellion collapsed.

Unfortunately, Henry III would prove to be as weak a ruler as his father had been cruel. War would come again to Kent and to Rochester.

An infantryman from about the time of the first seige. His basic equipment of helmet, shield and spear did not change much between about 1000 and 1250.

4. Continue south along Boley Hill to where Baker's Walk runs off to the right alongside the castle walls. Turn right down Baker's Walk to emerge on the river bank. Turn right. Continue along the river until you reach where the A229 carries its load of thundering traffic over the Medway. Behind you is the main gate into the outer bailey of the castle. You can enter the castle here free of charge to explore the ruins.

By 1264 King Henry III's financial incompetence had reduced the English government to bankruptcy. Unjust and illegal taxes were demanded to pay the bills while the corruption and favouritism went unchecked. Then Simon de Montfort, Earl of Leicester, stepped forward. He had won a great reputation for bravery and military skill fighting against the forces of Islam on Crusade, and was moreover a famously honest and competent nobleman when it came to money.

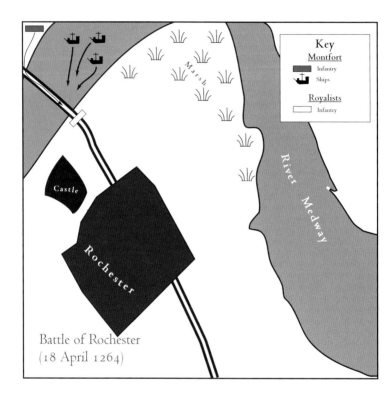

Battle of Rochester
(18 April 1264)

Key

Montfort

Infantry

Ships

Royalists

Infantry

When Montfort openly condemned Henry's government, men flocked to his standard and the earl suddenly found himself at the head of a popular uprising. City after city, nobleman after nobleman declared for Montfort and the cause of reformed government. Only a few places held out for the king. Among them was Rochester.

On 17 April 1264, Montfort and his army arrived on the west bank of the Medway. The castle and city were both held by professional soldiers, and the bridge was heavily barricaded and manned by armed guards. Montfort spent a day studying the situation, then ordered his men to make camp.

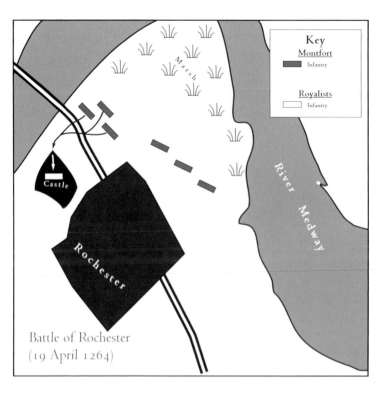

Battle of Rochester
(19 April 1264)

Next morning, while most of the baron's army gave every
impression of sleeping and resting, one party was sent galloping
downstream to Upnor while another grabbed their weapons and hid
near the bridge. At Upnor the men stole some fishing boats and
packed them with straw, wool and other combustibles. The men
then sailed the boats upstream to the bridge. As the boats
approached, they were set on fire. The straw and wool produced
vast clouds of dense, choking smoke that drifted over the bridge, its
barricades and its defenders. Under cover of the smoke, the men in
hiding leapt out and stormed forward. The bridge fell in minutes.

Montfort was not a man to pause. Next day he stormed the gatehouse, crashing through and capturing the outer bailey beyond. That left the keep holding out for the king. Unlike John, Montfort had no specialist German miners in his army. For a week Montfort and his army gazed at the keep wondering how to capture it.

Then dramatic news reached Montfort. King Henry had raised an army and was marching to capture London, financial heart of Montfort's cause. The royal army was then at Lewes. Again Montfort did not hesitate, but abandoned the siege and marched directly toward Lewes.

While at the bridge, it is worth crossing the A2 to look at the stretch of the river downstream of the bridge. In 1667 England was at war with Holland due to a trade dispute on the high seas. The war was not going well for England due largely to a financial crisis that meant the government could afford neither to repair damage to its warships nor pay the crews. Most ships of the Royal Navy were laid up in Chatham awaiting the money to get them repaired and sent to sea.

On 10 June the Dutch fleet suddenly appeared in the Thames estuary. Led by Admiral Michiel de Ruyter the Dutch first captured the fort at Sheerness then occupied the Isle of Grain, thus securing the entrance to the Medway. Two days later the Dutch ships pushed on up river to arrive off Chatham, which they proceeded to bombard. The next morning boarding parties were sent ashore to seize and burn three ships of the line. Smaller Dutch warships pushed up to the Rochester Bridge, but were driven off by canon-fire from the shore. On their way back downstream, the Dutch captured two English warships, including the fleet flagship *Royal Charles*. They escaped without loss.

Almost three centuries later, in May 1940, the Dutch war fleet fled its home ports to avoid being captured by the rapidly advancing panzers of Hitler's Wehrmacht. They headed for Britain to continue the struggle as the Free Dutch Navy and were ordered by the Royal Navy to put into Chatham as a temporary base. As they approached the port the Dutch admiral aboard his flagship de Ruyter radioed to the port commander: 'De Ruyter approaching Chatham.' 'Good God. Not again,' came the reply.

5. **Turn right to walk along the A229 for 100 yards, then bear right into the old High Street. Retrace your steps along the High Street, and so return to the railway station.**

◁ The ruined gate that gives access from the castle to the riverside. It was this gate that was attacked by the rebel forces of Simon de Montfort during the second siege. In 1264 it was protected by flanking towers, now vanished.

The walk starts at the Gatehouse of Lewes Castle, from which the knights loyal to Henry III issued to begin their assault on the rebel army.

9. LEWES
1264

Distance:	6 miles.
Terrain:	Mostly over surfaced paths, though the stretch down to Offham is unsurfaced and can be muddy after rain. The spur down to Offham is very steep, though short.
Public Transport:	Lewes is served by mainline railway and numerous bus routes.
Parking:	Several off-street car parks in the town.
Refreshments:	Numerous pubs, cafes and restaurants in Lewes, as well as shops that sell snacks and soft drinks.

While Simon de Montfort, Earl of Leicester, had been busy at the siege of Rochester, Henry III had been rebuilding the loyalties that his arrogant behaviour and reckless spending had lost him among the people of England. He was not, it must be said, terribly success-ful. Most of the towns and shires stayed loyal to Montfort and the cause of honest, efficient government.

But although Henry was shifty and untrustworthy as a man, as well as ineffective as a monarch, he was both ruthless and cunning. He turned to the higher nobility, telling them that Montfort wanted to put merchants and farmers in charge of the kingdom. Those he could not persuade, he bribed or bullied. By late April 1264 Henry had both caused many nobles to defect from the rebel cause, and raised an army of his own. He decided to gather his army in Sussex, then march on London to bring his rebellious capital to heel before marching down to crush Montfort between his army and the stout walls of Rochester.

Montfort moved too fast for him and on 12 May the scouts of the two armies clashed at the village of Offham. The royal army was camped in and around Lewes, that of Montfort at Fletching some nine miles north. Montfort sent a message to the king asking for peace, but laying down the strictest of terms: that Henry had to dismiss all his ministers and advisors so that they could be replaced by men chosen by Montfort. Henry refused in curt language, stating 'We value not your faith nor love and defy you as our enemy.' Henry's brother, Richard Earl of Cornwall, added in his own hand 'We let you know that you are defied as public enemies and that henceforth whenever occasion offers we will with all our might labour to damage your persons and your properties.'

At dawn next morning Montfort woke his army to hear mass and have their souls absolved of sin by the Bishop of Worcester, who was acting as the spiritual leader of the rebellion. He then had every man given a small cloth patch marked with a white cross and ordered it to be pinned to their clothing. Then, as the sun climbed over the eastern horizon, the rebel army headed for Lewes.

In Lewes, King Henry had been up late discussing things with his son, the twenty-five-year-old Edward, who would later become King Edward I. Also present was the king's brother, Richard of Cornwall, and other noblemen. They agreed that they should leave next morning to march on the rebels and destroy them. There was no sense of urgency for it seems to have been assumed that Montfort would remain at Fletching, or perhaps retreat to London. Still, there was no point taking chances so a scout was put on top of Offham Hill to the north of the town – where the racecourse now stands – to watch the road from Fletching.

Then the royal army went to bed. Prince Edward was staying in Lewes Castle while most of the nobles and knights found lodgings in the town. King Henry and his brother, meanwhile, were staying in the luxurious guest chambers at St Pancras Priory just to the south of the town. The bulk of the infantry and mustered feudal levy were camped in the fields and meadows around the priory.

A knight from the later thirteenth century. His mail armour completely covers his body while the head is protected by a helmet of thick iron.

At this date military technology had moved on somewhat from the days of Hastings, but tactics had not changed greatly from those employed by William the Conqueror in 1066. Infantry were still expected to play a secondary role in open battle. They were expected to defend hedges, walls and streams so as to block them to enemy advances. Formed in a dense phalanx, not unlike the old English shieldwall, the infantry could fight against other infantry units.

The key offensive tactic available to a commander was the charge of the heavily armed and armoured knights and men at

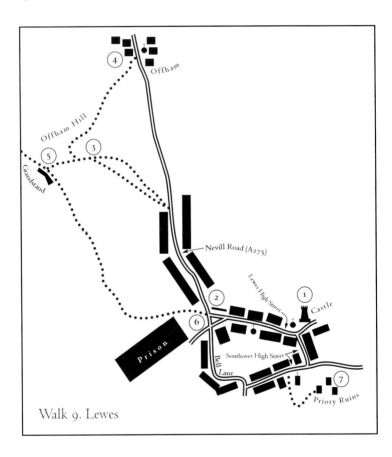

Walk 9. Lewes

arms. By 1264 these men were entirely encased in mail armour, with mail-covered gauntlets protecting their hands and even mail boots over their feet. The head was now protected by a helmet called the great helm, a solid iron affair that entirely encased the head, with holes for the eyes and for breathing. When charging a knight couched his lance, now longer and heavier than in 1066, so that it had the full weight of man and horse behind it. Once the

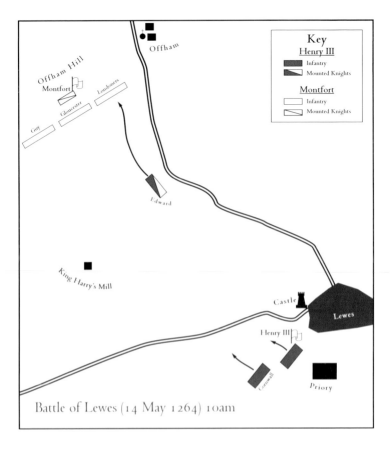

Key

Henry III
- ▰ Infantry
- ◣ Mounted Knights

Montfort
- ▱ Infantry
- ▱ Mounted Knights

Offham

Offham Hill

Montfort

Londoners

Guy

Gloucester

Edward

King Harry's Mill

Castle

Lewes

Henry III

Cornwall

Priory

Battle of Lewes (14 May 1264) 10am

initial impact had taken place, charging knights usually threw aside their lances – which were often broken in any case – in favour of the sword or mace. Close combat would then ensue until one side fled.

The battle that was to take place at Lewes would reveal two very different ways of combining infantry and armoured knights on the battlefield.

△ The summit of Offham Hill looking east from the position of the rebel right wing toward the position occupied by the Londoners.

▷ The steep chalk scree that lies just behind the position taken up by the Londoners at the start of the battle. It was down this slope that the Londoners retreated, with the knights led by Prince Edward in hot pursuit. Both units tumbled down the slope in great disorder.

THE WALK

1. From Lewes Castle, turn right into Lewes High Street, which soon becomes Western Road.

It was at about 8.30 on the morning of 14 May that a rider came clattering up this street, then paved with cobblestones. He hauled his horse to a halt just in front of the castle gates and shouted loudly to be admitted.

This rider was not the look-out left up on Offham Hill by the king the previous evening, as he had fallen fast asleep just before dawn and was now being rudely awoken by the swords of the rebels. The man in such a hurry was one of half a dozen men sent out with a cart by Prince Edward to cut grass from the smooth downs north of the town to feed the horses belonging to the knights staying in the town. These men had been on Mount Harry, a mile or so north-west of Offham Hill when they had seen a column of armed men marching into Offham along the road from Fletching, then turning to climb up Offham Hill.

Abandoning their cart, the men had taken to their horses and ridden in a sweeping curve to stay out of sight of the men arriving on Offham Hill. Presumably they emerged through Houndean Bottom, where Lewes Prison now stands, and so reached the castle.

Prince Edward was already awake, but was taking a leisurely breakfast in comfortable clothes and had neither his armour nor horse to hand. He quickly climbed up to the battlements of the castle keep, from where he could get a clear view of Offham Hill. Sure enough the army of Montfort was drawing itself up on the crest of the hill with banners unfurled.

Young Edward was capable and courageous, but he was also a famous drinker and had a savage temper. Whether he was angry or hungover at this moment we don't know, but it was here in

Lewes Castle that he made a mistake with far reaching consequences. He sent his servants to find his horse and armour and to wake every knight and nobleman in Lewes Castle and Lewes Town. What Edward did not do was send somebody to tell his father, the king, that Montfort was on Offham Hill. So while the castle and town hummed into life as men grabbed their weapons and horses, Henry III quietly went to join the monks in one of the many services that punctuated the monastic day in the thirteenth century. Some of the king's men heard the bustle in the town, but none of them thought it important enough to interrupt the king at his prayers.

At about 9.30am Edward led his force of knights and nobles out of the West Gate of Lewes and along what is now Western Road. Only then did Edward think to find out what the army's commander was doing. Looking south to the main camp around St Pancras Priory, Edward saw that the bulk of the infantry was arrayed and armed ready for battle. Assuming that King Henry had been alerted to Montfort's arrival and was, like Edward himself, about to advance, the young prince put his spurs to his horse and led his force of armoured knights north west.

In fact, Henry had only just emerged from the priory church. The infantry and their immediate commanders had seen Montfort's army and had themselves taken the precaution of arming and getting into formation. Henry saw his son ride out of Lewes and assumed that he would wait for orders before doing anything. Henry was both startled and furious when he saw his son set off towards the rebel army. He hurried to grab his weapons and start issuing orders.

2. At the end of Western Road, turn right into Nevill Road, the A275. At the point where Nevill Road leaves the cluster of housing estates that spread out from Lewes to the north a

gate on the left gives access to a track that leads up to the old racecourse. The track soon divides in two, take the right hand track.

This is almost certainly the route taken by Edward and his knights. As Edward led his men up the slope at a gentle trot, he realised that Montfort's left wing was occupied by the London militia and a mass of armed London citizens. A few weeks earlier Edward's mother, Queen Eleanor had been staying in the Tower of London when a pro-Montfort demonstration turned into an anti-Henry riot. Wanting to get the queen away from any danger, the Constable of the Tower put her in a barge surrounded by armed men and gave orders to the oarsmen to take her upstream to Windsor, where Edward was in residence. The mob saw the move and raced to London Bridge. As the barge passed underneath the mob shouted insults at Queen Eleanor, and one apprentice boy tipped over the parapet the contents of a chamberpot. Some of the filth splashed on to the queen's dress. When she arrived at Windsor and showed Edward what had happened, he was furious.

That fury was now rekindled, so Edward diverted the line of his advance. He bore away from the centre of the rebel army and turned right to attack the Londoners. The core of this rebel division was the well armed and well trained London militia in their distinctive striped outfits, but the bulk of the men were only ordinary citizens who had picked up knives, axes or other weapons as they left home.

Unsurprisingly the sight of a concentrated mass of heavily armoured knights heading straight at them unnerved the Londoners. When Edward gave his war cry and spurred his mount into a gallop, just 100 yards from the waiting Londoners it was too much. The Londoners turned and fled. Edward and his knights were in hot pursuit.

3. Where the track to the racecourse bends left, take the footpath through a gate on the right and follow the edge of the field. At the second gate, turn right through the gate and walk across the open grass to where a gate leads into woodland. Follow the path beyond the gate and through woodland down to Offham.

It was down this steep hill that the Londoners ran on foot, and Edward and his men chased them on horseback. Several of the horses took a tumble here, throwing their riders down the slope. But enough of them kept their footing to harry the fleeing rebels mercilessly.

At the foot of the hill, probably just outside Offham Church, Edward came across a most bizarre vehicle. It was a large farm cart that had a padded chair set on top of it on a wooden platform. Around the chair were scattered various writing desks and several piles of paper. Unknown to Edward, Montfort had broken his leg and this weird contraption was the mobile command headquarters of the rebel army, which Montfort could survey and control from his elevated chair. Montfort was now, of course, with his army. Edward and his men passed by the cart, seeking out vengeance on the fleeing Londoners. Both fugitives and hunters spread out and scattered across the flat lands of the Ouse Valley to the north.

4. Return up the hill to the original track. Turn right. Where the track leaves a thicket is a broad expanse of open grassland. This marked the centre of Montfort's position. Look south to see a long gentle slope leading down to Lewes.

While the Londoners were running north, the rest of Montfort's army stood calmly in position here. In what had been the centre, but since the collapse of the Londoners was now the left flank, was a division commanded by the youthful Earl of

The view from Montfort's position toward Lewes Castle. The houses in the foreground were not then in existence and open grassland extended right to the castle. It was along this route that the knights led by Prince Edward charged.

The view from Montfort's position toward the priory, which is hidden from view in the valley beyond the distant line of trees. It was up this slope that the king's division and that led by the Earl of Cornwall advanced. The walk goes down this hill following the wire fence visible on the right of the photograph.

The priory ruins in Lewes. King Henry III started and ended the battle here, and it was from this priory that he emerged to surrender to the rebels the following morning.

Gloucester. Gloucester was the only senior nobleman still fighting on Montfort's side. His division was composed largely of his own retainers and supporters. To his right was a division made up of mixed forces commanded by Henry de Montfort, Simon's son.

Simon himself had positioned himself behind Gloucester. With difficulty he had clambered on to the back of a horse, though he was incapable of riding at a pace faster than a walk. Under his own command Montfort had the small force of mounted and armoured knights who were with the rebels.

As Edward's knights disappeared from view over the crest of the hill, King Henry was hurrying north from the priory with his infantry. The royalist men were divided into two divisions, one led

The Battle of Lewes as depicted on one of the fine bronze panels attached to the battlefield monument that stands in the priory grounds. The scene shows the decisive attack by the rebel knights on the flank of the king's division.

by the king himself on the right and a second commanded by his brother Richard of Cornwall on the left.

It took the royal infantry about 20 minutes to get up the slope, they then paused for a short time to get back into order before launching their attack. Henry must have been hoping that at any moment Edward's knights would reappear over the hill to attack the rebels in the rear, but in fact the horsemen were by now some two miles away still cutting down the Londoners. Nevertheless the royal attack began well. Gloucester's men were pushed back slightly, though Henry de Montfort's men held firm.

Hand-to-hand combat continued for some time as casualties mounted, but neither side could gain an advantage. Eventually

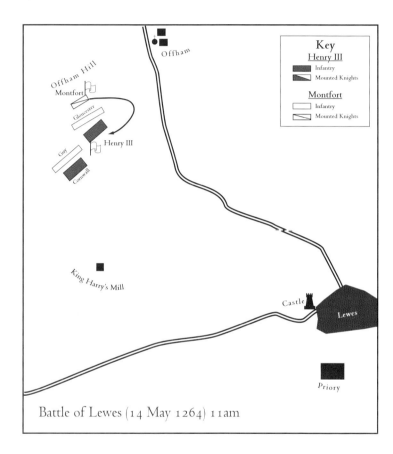

Battle of Lewes (14 May 1264) 11am

Richard of Cornwall's men began to fall back in the face of the younger Montfort's division. The king's division began to find its left flank coming under attack by some of Gloucester's men who edged around to their right. It was the type of opportunity for which Simon de Montfort had been waiting.

Montfort ordered the rebel knights to move to their left, trot-ting over the ground recently vacated by the Londoners, then to

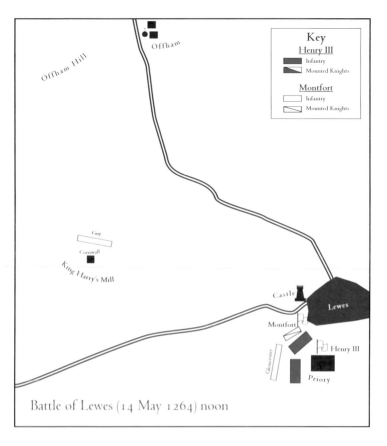

Battle of Lewes (14 May 1264) noon

wheel right and charge into the exposed right flank of Henry's division. Henry pushed forward to meet the threat, but his horse was killed and he tumbled to the ground. A knight gave up his horse to the king and Henry was soon back in the saddle, but it was too late. Assaulted on both flanks and no longer able to see their monarch, Henry's division broke and fled back down the slope.

5. Continue on along the track to reach the old racecourse grandstand. This is the approximate position of the right wing of Montfort's army. Turn left in front of the grandstand. Walk down the long grassy slope toward the distant bulk of Lewes Prison.

Although the king's division, and Henry himself, were making back towards Lewes with all speed, Richard of Cornwall's men were still fighting. Cornwall now carried out a most difficult manoeuvre under tricky circumstances. He ordered his men to march backward while still fighting, hoping to conduct an orderly withdrawal and so keep Montfort's men in play until Edward and his knights got back.

About two thirds of the way down this slope there stood in 1264 a windmill called King Harry's Mill. It was near here that Cornwall's division finally broke up and fled. Earl Richard himself clambered into the mill, pulling up the ladder after him. A mass of the younger Montfort's men gathered around the mill. They could not get in, and Earl Richard was certainly not coming out. The rebels settled down to shout insults and sing bawdy songs about millers to the isolated earl.

Meanwhile, the battle was entering its final phase.

6. Follow the path as it bends left in front of the prison to emerge back at the junction of Western Road and Nevill Road. Turn right to head due south into Bell Lane. This lane twists left, right. As it turn right Southover High Street branches off to the left heading east. Turn left into the High Street. After 300 yards turn right down Cockshill Road, signposted to Priory Ruins. After passing the railway, turn left along a path to enter the priory ruins. The monument to the battle, erected in 1964, stands just beyond the ruins.

While Cornwall had been fighting his slow retreat, Henry had reached St Pancras Priory. It was now about noon. Realising that the rebel army had called off its pursuit to concentrate on his brother's forces, Henry set about organising a last ditch defence of the priory. Most of his men had fled, but the king still had enough men to barricade the gates and hurriedly line the wall that ran around the priory gardens.

Once Cornwall was in his windmill and his men in flight, Montfort turned his attentions back to the king. By the time Montfort reached the priory gates, riding painfully on his horse, his men were being drawn up ready for the final assault. The rebels so outnumbered the royalists by this point that the attack could only succeed, with bloody results.

Montfort called off his men, sending them back some yards. He then rode up to the gates all smiles and politeness to ask if he could talk to his sovereign lord the king.

At this delicate moment, young Prince Edward and his knights rode back on to the crest of the hill over which they had disappeared some two hours earlier. Henry saw their banners and glittering armour, and promptly refused to meet with Montfort.

Warily Montfort turned to look back up the slope, a view now obscured by modern buildings. Edward and his men were making no attempt to advance. The young prince scanned the battlefield and realised what had happened. He was uncertain whether to attack, or whether he should lead his knights off to form the core of a new royalist army and fight another day.

In the event, the decision was made for him. As dusk fell the royalist knights began to slip away. Many of them had some sympathy with what Montfort was trying to achieve, others simply did not fancy the odds now against them. Whatever the reason by midnight Edward had barely a hundred men with him. He led them down to Lewes by a circuitous route and managed to get into the town.

7. Return to Southover High Street. Turn right. After about 100 yards the Southover High Street turns left, though it looks as if the main road goes straight on. Turn left here to return to Lewes High Street and so to the castle.

Now back at the castle, Edward sent a message to his father explaining what had happened. He received a curt and angry reply from the king stating the obvious, that they now had no choice but to surrender. At dawn next day both castle and priory opened their gates.

The results of the Battle of Lewes were far reaching and are with us today. Montfort's first move was to get the king to sign the document known as the Mise of Lewes. This established that the king could rule only with the agreement of a Council made up of noblemen and chaired by the highly respected, and very neutral, Bishop of Rouen. This Council in turn was expected to consult with Parliament. This institution had been in existence for some time, but had previously been made up of nobles and bishops only. Montfort now included in it commoners who were representing the various cities and shires of England. Working together, the Parliament and Council drew up reforms and measures to rid the government of corruption and get the royal finances back on a firm footing.

Montfort was later overthrown and killed, but his reforms survived him. The impetuous young Edward who had lost at Lewes saw Montfort's system in action. When he became king, Edward altered the system to give more power to the monarch, but he kept in place the idea of a Parliament representing the commoners as well as the nobility. That Parliament is with us still.

Lewes battlefield monument stands in the priory grounds, just east of the ruins. It was erected in 1964 to commemorate the 700th anniversary of the battle and takes the form of a contemporary helmet to which are attached a number of bronze reliefs.

Simon de Montfort, Earl of Leicester, the leader of the rebel forces at the Battle of Lewes as shown on one of the panels attached to the battlefield monument

10. ROTTINGDEAN
1377

Distance:	1 mile.
Terrain:	This walk is partly over surfaced paths and partly over open grassland. The route takes in one hill, though it is not too steep.
Public Transport:	Brighton & Hove Bus and Coach Company route 12 runs from Brighton to Eastbourne via Rottingdean.
Parking:	On-street parking in the village.
Refreshments:	Four pubs in Rottingdean and one shop that sells snacks and soft drinks.

In 1377 England and France were locked deep in the Hundred Years War, then some forty years old. Neither side had yet achieved a decisive advantage, though English armies were regularly campaigning in France. In the spring of that year the French decided to take the war to England, and the Battle of Rottingdean was the result.

King Charles V of France had thirty-five warships, to which he added eight Castillian galleys under the command of the mercenary captain Don Fernao Sanchez de Tovar. Promising easy access to English loot, Charles asked his merchants and fishermen to provide additional ships – and probably around 120 vessels turned up. The whole fleet, plus some 4,000 soldiers were put under the command of the experienced admiral Jean de Vienne. This Vienne put aside the flag of France and adopted a pirate's flag, for England and France were in the middle of a two year truce at the time and King Charles wanted to keep his hands clean.

The fleet left Harfleur late in June and sailed to Rye. Putting into the port under the guise of merchants, an advance guard seized

The beach at Rottingdean. The French fleet anchored just off shore while the soldiers streamed ashore. The slipway is modern, but stands on the site of the older structure.

The Rottingdean Windmill is a famous landmark on the coast road, now the A259, east of Brighton. At the time of the battle windmills were only just being introduced to Britain and although one stood here a few years later it is unclear if the downs had a mill on the day of battle.

the key gate, after which the rest of the 'pirate' fleet arrived. The citizens of Rye fled without fighting, taking all the valuables they could carry. Having stolen everything they could find, the French set fire to Rye and put to sea in search of other victims. The countryside had, by this time, been alerted. A raid of Winchelsea ended in failure as the defences were fully manned.

In early July, the date is not clear, Jean de Vienne arrived off Rottingdean. As soon as the ships were sighted, the residents began to flee, grabbing whatever they could carry as they raced inland. It was about noon.

THE WALK

1. In Rottingdean find the short section of High Street south of the A259 that runs down to the sea. Walk to the end of this road where a slipway leads down to where the sea laps the shore.

It was the fact that there was a narrow gap in the towering chalk cliffs here that had attracted Jean de Vienne. It meant that he would be able to land his men and march inland. The leading French troops landed and started to move north. They were at once met by a volley of archery. The men of Rottingdean were competent bowmen and were determined to slow the French advance so that their women and children could get away.

2. At the busy junction of the High Street with the A259, cross the main road with care and continue north-west up the High Street. Just beyond the crossroads with Steyning Road and Nevill Road, bear right into The Green to reach the parish church.

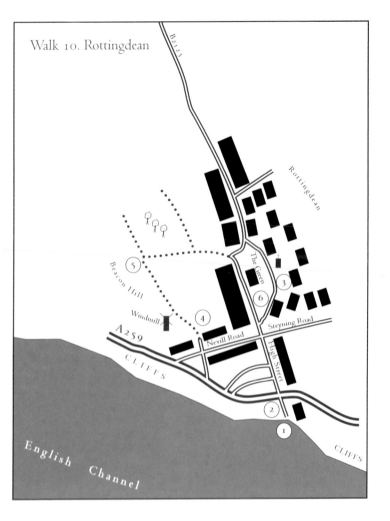

Walk 10. Rottingdean

It was up this road that the French advanced as the Englishmen fell back. As soon as the last of the families were seen to have got away up what is now the B2123, the local men fled. Their job was

The view down into Rottingdean from the summit of Beacon Hill. Assuming the French launched their ambush from here, they would have seen the English marching in from the left and pausing in front of the church.

Looking back down Beacon Hill toward the beach. The paths over the downs are here easy to follow for they are mown short by the Council.

done. One man, mounted on a local horse, was sent at high speed to Lewes.

The French, meanwhile, were getting ashore in numbers. The houses of the village were ransacked, then set on fire. The Church of St Margaret was also set on fire. It was at this date about 500 years old, with some recent additions such as a modern tower. The flames were intensely fierce, destroying the roof completely. Three of the pillars at the west end of the nave still show scorch marks caused by this fire. The church as it stands today is the Victorian restoration of the structure built in the 1390s, with only the tower remaining of what was here in 1377.

By late afternoon the main French force was ashore and Jean de Vienne was preparing to march inland on a raid intended to last all the following day. At this point one of his scouts came racing back down the road to announced that a force of 500 armed Englishmen was approaching.

This relief force was the local militia under the command of John de Caroloco, Prior of Lewes, supported by two local knights Sir John Falvesley and Sir Thomas Cheyne. The English were unaware of the true size of the French raiding force, thinking that they outnumbered the invaders when, in fact, they were outnumbered by around eight to one.

Vienne wasted little time making his arrangements to meet the English. He sent a small force of men north of the village to play the part of the small body of men the English were expecting to meet. Then he led his main force into position to spring an ambush.

3. From the church return to the Steyning Road crossroads and turn right into Nevill Road.

4. After about 100 yards Nevill Road meets Sheep Walk. Turn right. This road comes to a dead end, but a footpath

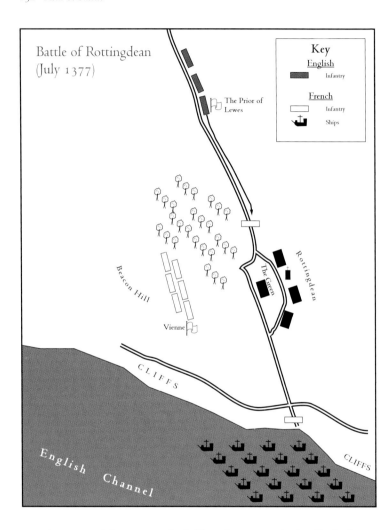

Battle of Rottingdean
(July 1377)

Key

English

Infantry

French

Infantry

Ships

The Prior of
Lewes

Beacon Hill

Vienne

The Green

Rottingdean

CLIFFS

CLIFFS

English Channel

continues straight on up the hill and past a windmill. A short
distance beyond the windmill the path meets another near the
top of Beacon Hill.

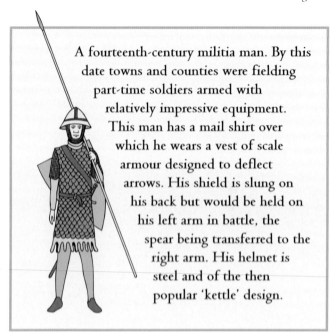

A fourteenth-century militia man. By this date towns and counties were fielding part-time soldiers armed with relatively impressive equipment. This man has a mail shirt over which he wears a vest of scale armour designed to deflect arrows. His shield is slung on his back but would be held on his left arm in battle, the spear being transferred to the right arm. His helmet is steel and of the then popular 'kettle' design.

It was probably here that Vienne drew up the bulk of his army. In 1377 the slopes of this hill were more wooded than they are today, so the Frenchmen would have been out of sight of the advancing English.

For some time Vienne and his men waited silently on this hill. They heard the English approaching, then the sounds of fighting as the decoy French force north of the village played their part. Feigning surprise and panic, the decoy force made a pretence of fighting, then turned to move rapidly south as if fleeing through the village to the waiting ships and safety. When they reached the beach a prearranged signal was given – perhaps a trumpet blast.

Vienne struck. He gave the order to his men to charge down the slope.

5. Turn right along the path that leads down Beacon Hill towards the village. This path emerges on to High Street. Turn right.

It was here that Vienne drew up his main force, facing south. The English were now caught in the narrow valley with the sea in front of them and Vienne behind. They had no intention of surrendering, however, so they turned to fight.

As the true size of the French force became clear, the English realised that they were in a hopeless position. Sir John Falvesley managed to cut his way out of the closing trap with a handful of men and raced inland to alert the defenders of Lewes. Prior John de Caroloco and Sir Thomas Cheyne were both captured, along with most of the Englishmen. About 100 men had been killed.

6. Continue south along High Street to return to the start of the walk.

Having defeated the local militia, Vienne was free to do what he liked for a few days until more Englishmen could be mustered and marched to face him. His first move was to march on Lewes. When he arrived there the day after the fight at Rottingdean he found the gates shut and the walls fully manned. He and his men occupied, looted and burned several nearby villages before returning to Rottingdean.

The French fleet left after staying off Rottingdean for about five days. They later moved on to Dover, but were driven off. The fleet returned to France in early September and was disbanded.

The pond on the green was constructed to gather water from the surrounding downs to provide drinking water for the village and its livestock. The fighting raged around The Green as the French sprung their ambush.

Rottingdean church is dedicated to St Michael. It was much restored in the nineteenth century, but the tower is thirteenth century and stood here on the day of battle. Rudyard Kipling was a regular worshipper here, prompting the Americans to build an exact copy of this church adorned with some of Kipling's poetry as the main chapel at the famous Forest Lawns Cemetery in Los Angeles, California.

11. SANDWICH
1460

For a thousand years the town of Sandwich was one of the most important ports in southern England. The two-mile-wide Wantsum Channel that separated Thanet from the mainland provided both a convenient shipping lane and safe anchorage for fleets. That channel began to dry up in around 1300 and by 1500 Sandwich harbour was accessible to the sea only along the River Stour. By 1700 the harbour could no longer be reached by sea-going ships and dealt only with local coasting trade and fishing boats.

The loss of the Wantsum Channel is conventionally blamed on silting, though there seems no clear reason why silt should have been more of a problem in 1400 than in 400. It may be that the sea levels dropped around this time due to the cooling of the world's climate that was then taking place. Even with modern global warming, the climate in England is still not as mild as it was before 1300.

As an important port, Sandwich became the focus for invaders and internal wars of all types. There was a land battle here between the English and Vikings in 850 and another in 991, naval battles took place in 1009 and 1048 while in 1217 a French invasion

△ The railway station at Sandwich where the walk starts and finishes. The walk leaves by way of a modern housing estate.

▷ The open ditch that formed the first line of defence to the town of Sandwich in medieval times. The wall originally stood along the top of the bank on the left of the picture, but only fragments now remain.

The section of town wall at the north-eastern corner of Sandwich old town area. The walls originally stood about 15 feet tall.

captured the town before being fought off with much bloodshed. However the landscape around the town has changed so much since these battles that it is now impossible to correlate the recorded events with any present day features.

The battle of 1460 was different for it took place in and around the town itself. The fight at Sandwich was the third outbreak of bloodshed in the Wars of the Roses. Although compared to later battles it was tiny in scale, its political ramifications were immense.

The dynastic and legal disputes in the Wars of the Roses were complex, but the key issues were clear cut. The unfortunate King Henry VI suffered bouts of forgetfulness and simple mindedness that grew increasingly severe and eventually bordered on madness. At such times his wife and her assorted aristocratic cronies plundered government funds for their own use, while degrading the

An archer from the Wars of the Roses. He wears a helmet and studded leather armour and carries a sword as well as his bow. Such men formed a major part of all armies of this period.

administration with corruption and favouritism. Opposition to Queen Margaret was led by the Duke of York. He spent the 1440s and 1450s in periodic political disputes.

In 1455 the political disputes led to a murderous brawl that historians with hindsight dignified with the name First Battle of St Albans. This gave York the upper hand, but in 1459 more fighting led to Yorkist victory at Blore Heath, which Queen Margaret rapidly overcame by getting the Yorkists legally branded as traitors and raising a large army in the name of Henry VI. Because Henry VI was the grandson of a Duke of Lancaster, the faction backing Queen Margaret became known as the Lancastrians.

York fled to Ireland while his son Edward, Earl of March and later King Edward IV, went with the main Yorkist ally the Earl of Warwick to Calais. Calais at this date belonged to England and was

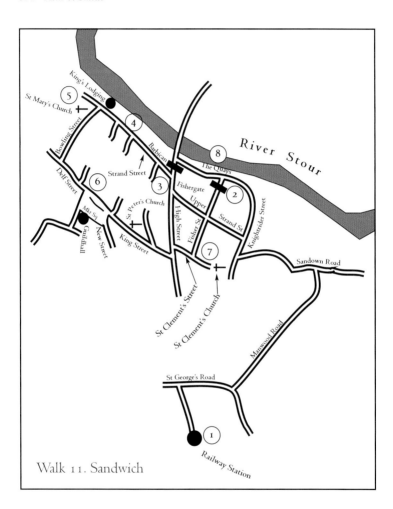

Walk 11. Sandwich

a major centre for the highly lucrative wool trade. By controlling Calais, Warwick and Edward had access to the wealth and huge stores of weapons in the town. Naturally Queen Margaret was determined to oust them. She ordered the mustering of a fleet and an army at Sandwich under the command of Sir Richard Woodville, Baron Rivers, with orders to attack Calais as soon as possible.

In the event, Warwick struck first.

THE WALK

1. In Sandwich find the railway station. The old town of Sandwich is a maze of narrow streets and alleys that can be confusing to the visitor. Whether you arrive by public transport or car, however, the station is well signposted. From the station follow the access road north-west to the junction with St George's Road. Turn right. Where St George's Road turns right, bear left into Manwood Road. At the far end of Manwood Road is a T-junction. Turn left. This road crosses a small bridge that spans the old town ditch with what remain of the original town walls beyond. The road ends in another T-junction. Turn right into Knightrider Street. This road soon bends left to become The Quays, with the River Stour on your right.

At 4am on 15 January 1460 the harbour staff on duty here saw a small fleet of ships coming up the River Stour. The ships moved slowly into what was then the extensive area of sheltered water known as Sandwich Basin, but which is now dry land beyond the Stour. If the men on the quays felt any anxiety about the new arrivals, they soon faded. The ships were well known in Sandwich being merchantmen engaged in the Baltic timber trade. What the Sandwich men did not know was that the timber ships had put into Calais a few days earlier and been promptly seized by the Earl of Warwick. The ships were now under Warwick's command and were packed with around 800 of his finest troops.

▷ The Fishergate, one of the original
medieval town gates of Sandwich. The
Yorkists gained access to the town through
this gateway as they launched their raid.

▽ A view along Strand Street.
Sandwich contains a greater concentration
of houses more than 200 years old than
any other town in the county.

After waiting in the Basin for about an hour, perhaps because of the tide, the ships warped into shore and tied up here along The Quays. Without warning hundreds of armed men surged down the gangplanks. The few men on duty were quickly overpowered. Sir John Dynham led a small body of Yorkists to seize the Fishergate which guarded the entrance to the town from the quayside.

The gate was occupied without trouble. The Fishergate which stands today is the same as the one attacked that morning, though the top storey was added a century later.

Warwick had with him a tailor, a butcher and an apothecary. All three men were Yorkist supporters who were natives of Sandwich and had crossed over to Calais only a couple of weeks earlier. The invaders now split up into four armed groups. Three of them headed into the town with one of the locals to show them the way. The fourth raced along the dockside to board and capture the Lancastrian ships tied up here.

The walk follows the route of the most important of the armed groups heading into the town.

2. Pass through the Fishergate and turn right into Upper Strand Street. At the far end of this street turn right into High Street.

3. In front of you is the Barbican, a massive artillery bastion built here to replace a medieval town gate by Henry VIII when he was worried about a possible French invasion. Turn left into Strand Street. Continue along Strand Street to reach the half-timbered mansion known as King's Lodging, now a private house.

This house, built in 1400, was the first target of the attackers. In 1460 the building belonged to Christchurch Abbey,

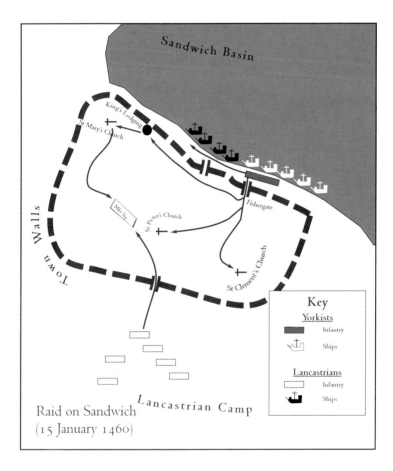

Sandwich Basin

King's Lodging

St Mary's Church

Town Walls

Mill St.

St Peter's Church

Fishergate

St Clement's Church

Key

Yorkists

Infantry

Ships

Lancastrians

Infantry

Ships

Lancastrian Camp

Raid on Sandwich
(15 January 1460)

Canterbury. It had been built to provide lodgings for foreign pilgrims landing at Sandwich and heading for Canterbury Cathedral, and included within it luxurious rooms for the use of visiting noblemen. It was here that the commander of the Lancastrian fleet, Baron Rivers, was lodging with his family.

So complete was the surprise achieved by Warwick's men that

Rivers was asleep in bed when the armed men kicked in his bedroom door and seized him. Rivers was dragged into the street in his nightshirt along with his wife and son. The three were hurriedly dragged off along Strand Street to the Yorkist ships where they were hustled below and locked in a cabin.

Meanwhile, the force that had occupied the King's Lodging was moving on.

4. Continue along Strand Street for a short distance past King's Lodging, then turn left into Bowling Street. On your right is St Mary's Church. Apart from lacking the tower, which collapsed in 1667, this church is little altered from how it appeared at the time of the Yorkist attack and is well worth a visit. It has what is reputed to be the finest and certainly the largest medieval roof in the county.

A key objective of the attackers was to seize the churches to stop the bells being rung to sound the alert. The principal objective was St Peter's Church in which hung the massive Curfew Bell. This church, which the walk will pass, was seized successfully but one other was not. This was most likely St Mary's as it was the furthest of the town churches from the Yorkist landing position.

As the bells from the now vanished tower boomed out, the raiders realised that they had lost the element of surprise.

5. Continue along Bowling Street to where it meets Delf Street at a T-junction. Turn left. If you wish you can bear right where Delf Street opens out into Market Square to visit the Tourist Information Centre which is housed in the sixteenth-century Guildhall. The building is worth a visit, but was not here in 1460.

As the Yorkists emerged into the Market Square they were met by a mass of armed Lancastrians pouring out of New Street, having raced into the town from their camp outside. The two parties of men flew at each other and savage hand-to-hand fighting raged. The Lancastrians had the advantage of numbers, but they lacked armour having been roused from their beds while the Yorkists were fully armoured and wide awake. After a while the Lancastrians were pushed back up New Street and out of the town.

6. Leave the square along King Street, passing St Peter's Church on your left by the junction with St Peter's Street. This ancient church is no longer a place of worship, but is open to the public and contains some fascinating historic items. At the end of King Street, turn left into High Street then first right to enter St Clement's Street. At the end of this lane is St Clement's Church. This is the oldest church in Sandwich, being the original parish church built when the local English were converted to Christianity in the seventh century. Most of the building is medieval, but Saxon fragments remain.

7. After visiting St Clement's, return to St Clement's Street, then turn north into Fisher Lane. Follow this lane north out of Fishergate and back on to The Quays.

Barely an hour after landing the Yorkist forces were gathering back on the dockside. The men were loaded back on to their ships, and on to the captured Lancastrian vessels. One of the captured ships was not ready for sea, so it was set on fire. The others were steered out on the tide, slipping downstream along the Stour to enter the Channel and so return to Calais.

▷ The King's Lodging House, which featured in the raid. It is now a private home and is not open to the public.

▽ The old Guildhall seen across Market Square. It was here that the sleepy garrison tried to muster to face the raiders.

▷ St Peter's Church, where the curfew and alarm bell was hung during medieval times. The brick upper parts of the tower date to after the time of the raid.

▽ St Peter's Church is no longer used for religious services and instead houses various historic items, such as this old horse-drawn fire engine from ninteenth-century Sandwich.

8. Turn right along The Quays and return to the railway station along the route by which you came.

The attack on Sandwich was small in scale, but immense in its impact. In the short term it exposed the incompetence of the government of Queen Margaret and encouraged the Yorkists. Margaret responded by giving orders to strengthen coastal defences against what she rightly thought would be an imminent invasion by York and Warwick. This had the effect of draining the royal coffers and made it impossible for Margaret to organise a proper resistance when York did invade that summer.

But it was the long term effects that nobody could have foreseen that had the greatest impact. Baron Rivers was kept a prisoner by Warwick in Calais, but was allowed to have his family with him. Among them was his young daughter Elizabeth Woodville. Edward, Earl of March, promptly fell in love with the girl and when he became king as Edward IV married her to make her his queen. The Woodvilles proved to be greedy and tactless in-laws for the king. It was largely their influence that drove many who loved Edward, but detested the Woodvilles to abandon Edward's brother Richard III and instead support the Tudors in 1485.

Thus did the small raid on Sandwich end up having profound dynastic impact more than twenty years later.

12. DEAL
1495 & 1648

Distance:	2 miles.
Terrain:	This bracing seaside walk is entirely over paved paths and includes no hills. If preferred, and tide and weather allow, some of the walk can be completed along Deal Beach.
Public Transport:	Deal is on the mainline railway.
Parking:	On-street parking in Deal.
Refreshments:	Several pubs and cafés in Deal, plus shops selling light snacks and soft drinks.

The Wars of the Roses are conventionally said to have ended in 1485 when the Yorkist King Richard III was killed at the Battle of Bosworth and the new Tudor Dynasty came to the throne in the form of Henry VII. However, the bloodshed and upheavals continued for some years after that, as the events at Deal in 1495 show.

Although Henry did his best to calm the rivalries and feuds that had erupted during the Wars of the Roses, it was inevitable that some were discontented with the new regime. In 1490 the lost cause of York seemed to have a chance of revival when a young man appeared in Burgundy and asked for an audience with Duchess Margaret, daughter of the late King Edward IV of England. The young man told the Duchess that he was her brother, Richard. Richard of York had been missing since 1483 when he and his brother, Edward V, were last seen in the none too gentle care of Richard III. Although many people assumed Richard had murdered the two boys, no bodies or real evidence had ever been found. The claimant told a tale of narrow escapes and subterfuge. Duchess Margaret declared herself convinced and threw herself into promoting the cause of her supposed brother.

The moat of Deal Castle is deep and broad. This was a revolutionary design when it was constructed on the orders of King Henry VIII. The walls of the inner fortress, to the right, were sunk deep in to the ground to shield them from incoming cannon balls while their sheer face on to the moat made them a formidable obstacle for assaulting enemy troops.

By 1495 several Irish lords had declared for 'Richard of York', as had King Charles VIII of France and King James IV of Scotland. Nobody in England had yet declared for the young man, but several Yorkist exiles joined the banner in Burgundy. Money was raised and mercenaries hired. In July 1495 'Richard of York' set out to invade England.

THE WALK

1. In Deal find the pier and the stretch of beach immediately to its south.

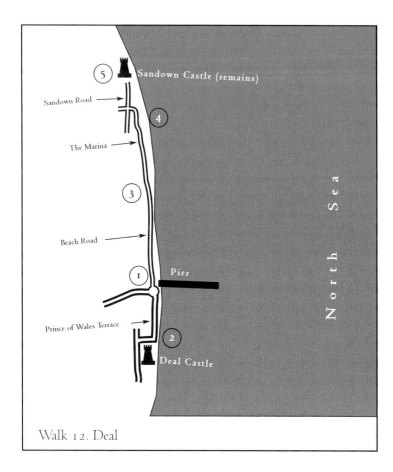

Walk 12. Deal

It was along this stretch of beach that the invaders chose to land and so begin the invasion of England. In 1495 neither the pier nor Deal Castle existed, while Deal itself was a small fishing village of scattered cottages.

The fleet provided by Burgundy anchored off shore while a small force of mounted scouts were sent ashore to ride out to survey

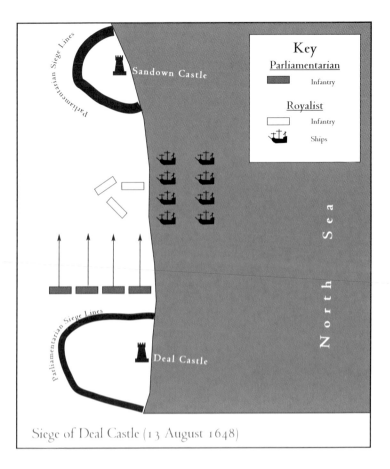

Siege of Deal Castle (13 August 1648)

the surrounding countryside. They were followed by a hundred or so infantry, who began to construct entrenchments and breastworks to serve as a base for the army. The site of the camp has been lost in the subsequent development of Deal, but may have stood somewhere near the roundabout where the A258 goes inland.

Suddenly the scouts came dashing back to camp with news that

The main entrance to Deal Castle. The apparently solid approach way has a removable section close to the gate to protect it if the castle came under attack.

Local fishing boats pulled up on Deal Beach. During the Tudor uprising the assaulting soldiers scrambled ashore from craft that had been beached, just as these have been.

a large column of infantry was approaching from the west along the road that led to Canterbury. Guessing that this was the local Kent militia coming to contest the landing, 'Richard of York' ordered those men already ashore to stand to arms to guard the half-built fortifications. Those still on board ship were told to stand by for instant landing if needed, while the boats were prepared to either land new troops or evacuate those ashore as events demanded.

The Kent militia, for it was indeed this body of troops that was approaching, moved quickly. They marched up to reach within about 300 yards of the entrenchments, then deployed into line and attacked. The fighting was short and sharp, and very decisive. Within less than ten minutes the invaders were running to the beach to reach their boats and be taken off.

The projected invasion of 'Richard of York' was over. He would try again in Devon a couple of years later and achieve rather greater success. But when the pretender was unmasked as being Perkin Warbeck, the son of a Flemish merchant, his support fell apart. Some people have theorised that he may have owed his striking similarity to the Yorkist family to the fact that he was an illegitimate son of the notorious womaniser Edward IV.

2. From the pier walk south along Prince of Wales Terrace until that road bends sharp right. In front of you is Deal Castle. The Castle is open to the public and contains much to see. There is an admission charge. If you wish to visit the castle, do so at this point then return to the southern end of Prince of Wales Terrace.

The castle was built as a platform for the then new-fangled cannon by King Henry VIII in the sixteenth century when England was facing a possible French invasion. The invasion never

A cavalryman from the early Tudor period, a number of the Kent militia who fought at Deal in 1495 would have been armed like this. He wears a metal helmet and has a mail shirt covered by leather armour. His legs are protected by sheets of plate steel. He carries a lance for use on horseback and a sword for when fighting on foot.

materialised, so it was not until the English Civil War that Deal Castle saw any action.

By 1648 King Charles I had been captured by the Parliamentarian army and was being held prisoner on the Isle of Wight. Despite this, the war dragged on. The English war fleet anchored just off Deal, having so far remained neutral, suddenly declared for the king. Marines were put ashore to seize the three castle of Deal, Sandown and Walmer. Parliament was not slow to respond and in June an army led by Colonel Rich arrived at Deal.

Rich had a difficult task for the Royalists could keep the castles supplied by sea, and could even move men from one to the other whenever an attack looked imminent. Nevertheless, Rich was a professional and experienced soldier. He quickly realised that Deal was the strongest of the three and Walmer the weakest, at least when attacked by land. He therefore began at Walmer, building entrenchments around the fortress and bringing up cannon to pound the walls. The Royalists were under no illusions as the strength of Walmer. As soon as an assault looked likely they evacuated the place by sea.

On 13 July, Rich moved against Deal and Sandown. Again he began by digging entrenchments around the fortresses to isolate them from the land, and then began preparing emplacements for his siege artillery. Although Rich kept up a pretence of besieging both castles, he did not in fact have enough men to man two sets of siege works properly. He decided to concentrate on Deal.

By 13 August the siege works around Deal Castle were almost complete. It was clear that the artillery barrage was about to begin. The Royalists decided to strike first.

3. Return north along Prince of Wales Terrace to pass the pier. At the roundabout continue north along the beach walking up Beach Road. After about 600 yards you will find Gold Street and Silver Street on your left.

It was in about this spot that on the night of 13 August that 800 men were landed from Royalist ships. Their mission was to move inland as quietly as possible, then swing south to approach the Roundhead siege works from behind. They were to assault the lines, spike the guns and then dash into Deal Castle.

Unfortunately for the Royalists, one of their sentries in Deal that evening decided that the king's cause was lost. As soon as it was dark he abandoned his position and crept over no-man's land to the enemy lines. He was taken to see Colonel Rich and betrayed the plan. This gave Rich just enough time to move a force of men out of the siege lines and get them lined up in battle formation.

Rich marched his men north, coming upon the Royalists before they had had time to form up after disembarking on the beach. There was a short and rather confused battle along the beach and in the area of what are now Gold Street and Silver Street. The smoke added to the confusion of gun flashes in the dark. The Royalists were soon hopelessly muddled. Some scrambled back into their boats on the beach, others headed north.

4. Continue north along Beach Road, which soon becomes The Marina. When The Marina turns sharp left away from the beach, follow it and then take the first right into Sandown Road. At the end of this road lie the remains of Sandown Castle – though in truth there is little left to see.

The Royalist fugitives from the night action ran up this approach road and into Sandown Castle. There they slammed the gates behind them, isolating the pursuing Roundheads on the sandy flats where the houses lining Sandown Road have since been built.

The abortive raid proved to be the Royalists last effort in Kent. On 23 August news arrived that the main Royalist army had been utterly defeated at the Battle of Preston in distant Lancashire a few days earlier. The garrison of Deal Castle surrendered at once, that in Sandown Castle held out until 5 September.

The Civil War was over in Kent.

5. Retrace your steps along the coast road to the starting point of the walk.

The beach at Deal is long, straight and gently shelving. It made an ideal landing ground for the Civil War soldiers, and was earmarked for a similar role by the Germans in 1940.

The site of Sandown Castle is marked by these ornamental gardens, built into the meagre ruins of the old fortress. Sandown was built to a similar design to Deal, but was considerably smaller.

13. WROTHAM
1554

Distance:	4¼ miles.
Terrain:	This gentle walk over the lower slopes of the North Downs includes a section of the old Pilgrim's Way, now forming part of the North Downs Way long distance footpath.
Public Transport:	Wrotham is served by the Arriva Kent Thameside 308 bus from Sevenoaks.
Parking:	On-street parking in the village.
Refreshments:	Three pubs in Wrotham, plus a shop selling light snacks and soft drinks.

Warfare was changing rapidly in the mid-sixteenth century when the Battle of Wrotham was fought. For the past two centuries firearms had been large, cumbersome, unreliable and inaccurate. From around 1510 improvements in gunpowder and gun barrel manufacture was changing all that. Wrotham was one of the first battles on English soil where the new guns and new tactics developed to support them were put into practice.

The key weapon was the harquebus, a firearm that shot a ball weighing around 2 ounces over a distance of about 100 yards, though it was accurate over only half that distance. The weapon was fired with a fuse that remained alight even in damp weather. A trigger plunged this into a firing hole, which was covered by a small lid that pulling the trigger moved aside. These two key technical innovations combined with more reliable powder meant that the weapon could be loaded aimed and fired with some expectation that it would actually go off. This may not sound much, but compared to earlier firearms it was a great improvement.

Reloading the harquebus was a lengthy affair, taking over a

▷ The statue of St George that stands above the door of Wrotham Church. At the time of the battle, this niche would have been empty. The original medieval statue would have been destroyed during the Protestant reformation that was supported by the rebels, but which Queen Mary was attempting to eradicate. The current statue was installed during the later twentieth century.

▽ The road sign says it all. This section of the Pilgrim's Way is now occupied by a modern housing estate, but the site of the battle has been left undeveloped.

▷ Beyond the houses of Wrotham the Pilgrim's Way becomes a trackway that has altered relatively little since the day of the battle. This view is looking west. The royal army advanced down this section of track, then deployed to the left to occupy the hill crest to block the rebel advance.

▽ The view that would have been enjoyed by Lord Abergavenny on the day of the battle. The hedge to the right marks the course of the Pilgrim's way. The field to the left is where Abergavenny drew up his men. The rebels came over the distant ridge, then charged up the slope in the foreground.

minute. Commanders therefore drew their men up five or more ranks deep and had the ranks fire in turn, timing the volleys so that the first had reloaded by the time the last had fired. Even so the harquebusiers were vulnerable to sudden charges by cavalry or infantry armed with edged weapons. To protect them numbers of men with halbards were mixed in with the harquebusiers. By 1550 it had become conventional for the men to be drawn up in squares with the halbardiers grouped in the corners. This formation was called a hedgehog.

Marching over a battlefield in a tightly formed square called for a high degree of training. Only professional, or at least semi-professional, regiments and militias could hope to carry out these new tactics successfully. Warfare was becoming more a task for full time soldiers than amateur warriors, though this was not always appreciated at the time.

One man who did not fully appreciate the changing nature of warfare was Sir Thomas Wyatt. Poet and courtier, Wyatt was also an ardent Protestant at the time when the division of Europe into religious factions was causing widespread bloodshed on the continent. England had been largely spared the worst excesses of inter-communal religious violence, although there had been a number of executions under both Henry VIII and his Protestant son Edward VI. Generally, however, these were not so much for the religious views of the victims as for the trouble they tried to stir up.

In 1553 Edward died. An attempt was made to put his Protestant cousin Lady Jane Grey on the throne, but this was put down by Edward's Catholic sister Mary. Although Mary began introducing Catholic measures into the government of the largely Protestant England, peace continued to reign. Then, late in 1553, Mary announced that she was going to marry King Philip of Spain rather than one of the various English noblemen who thought themselves eligible. Philip was a strict Catholic who had persecuted

Protestants within his kingdom with the notorious Spanish Inquisition. Mary promised that such measures would not come to England, but Sir Thomas Wyatt and other leading Protestants did not believe her.

The Protestants began talking among themselves. Most favoured working with Mary and within the government to oppose any moves by Philip to introduce the Inquisition to England. Wyatt and a few others preferred to organise a rebellion. The date set for the uprising was 25 January 1554. The rebels fanned out through the country to organise the business.

Unfortunately for the rebels, few of their fellow Protestants were inclined to join them. Only in Kent, where Wyatt himself lived, did the uprising break out as planned. The rebels were to meet at Rochester, then march on London.

Mary's government had got wind of the planned rebellion from the failed efforts elsewhere and had sent Lord Abergavenny with 600 professional soldiers to Kent to keep an eye on things. Abergavenny and his men were resting in the village of Wrotham waiting for news when a scout came in from the west to announce the approach of a body of rebels led by Sir Henry Isley, a local landowner.

THE WALK

1. In Wrotham find the parish church. In 1554 this stood at the eastern end of the village. Abergavenny and his men were camped in the churchyard. Follow Abergavenny's advance by walking north past the church then turning left up Old London Road to reach a crossroads. Turn left into Pilgrim's Way. Where this road turns sharp left continue straight on along the well signposted North Downs Way. Once beyond

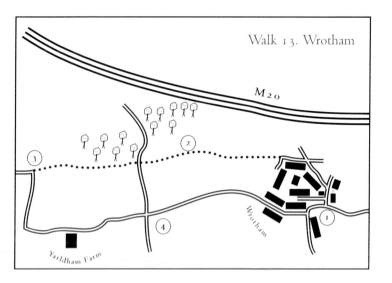

Walk 13. Wrotham

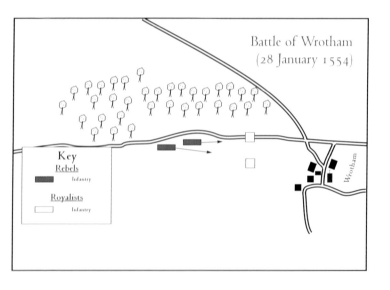

Battle of Wrotham
(28 January 1554)

▷ The walk follows the Pilgrim's Way to this point where the track crosses a surfaced lane. The Pilgrim's Way continues on west, as did the retreating rebels after the battle. The walk turns left down the slope to the south.

▽ The lane that runs back to Wrotham passes to the south of the battlefield, which lies behind the hedge on the left.

the houses you enter Blacksole Field, where most of the fighting took place.

Abergavenny drew his men up in the standard hedgehog formation, probably in two units astride the Pilgrim's Way as it crossed Blacksole Field. The advancing rebels were neither as well trained nor as well equipped as Abergavenny's men. Very few had firearms of any kind, most being armed with halbards, swords or axes. Sir Henry knew his 500 men could not hope to defeat the royalists if he adopted standard tactics. Instead he ordered his men to charge forward in their column of march in the hope that they would reach the enemy before they had time to form up properly.

The rebels ran forward across the Blacksole Field, but were not fast enough. Volley after volley of harquebus fire crashed out. Inaccurate the weapons may have been, but they inflicted casualties on the rebels. The attacking columns faltered, then halted.

Abergavenny ordered his men to advance at a steady pace, keeping formation and firing as they went. The rebels fell back, Sir Henry Isley desperately trying to rally them. About the position of the modern electricity pylons the rebels broke and fled back along the Pilgrim's Way. Abergavenny ordered his men to give chase.

2. Continue along the North Downs Way past the pylon, then across a surfaced lane and into a gravel track. Continue along this track, with a wood to your right, until you emerge on to a second surfaced lane.

At around this spot something quite extraordinary happened. Abergavenny was urging his men on to pursue and harry the rebels. He himself was leading they way, mercilessly hacking and thrusting at the rebels. As he brutally killed a wounded man lying on the

A harquebusier carries his heavy weapon ready for action. Most men had a wooden staff on which to rest the gun while firing.

ground Abergavenny suddenly noticed something was wrong. His men were not with him.

In fact the royalist troops had halted without orders and were standing around watching the rebels escape. As professional soldiers they had trained to fight foreign enemies. They had known the rebellion needed to be put down, of course, but many of the soldiers were Protestants who had no more regard for Philip of Spain than did Wyatt. They had broken the rebel force and knew that the poorly armed rebels would most likely slink off home. There was no reason, as they saw things, for the ruthless killing of men who were already beaten. The rebels were, after all, Englishmen like themselves.

Abergavenny was furious. He gathered his men together and marched them back along the Pilgrim's Way to Wrotham where he treated them to stern lectures on duty, loyalty and following orders. It was no good. That night several men deserted. Over the follow-ing days others slipped away, some of whom then joined Wyatt's

A halbardier, a type of soldier that took its name from his principal weapon. The task of these men was to protect the harquebusiers while they reloaded.

rebellion. Those who remained made it clear to Abergavenny that they would not carry out his more extreme orders.

Abergavenny trailed off back to Queen Mary in London to give her the news that the rebellion had not been crushed.

3. If you wish, you may return to Wrotham along the North Downs Way. Alternatively turn left along the surfaced lane. Follow it where it bends sharp left and runs east past Yarldham Farm.

4. At a crossroads continue straight on and so return to Wrotham village.

14. COOLING
1554

Distance:	3 miles.
Terrain:	A gentle walk over relatively flat land, mostly surfaced or gravel tracks with no steep hills or difficult terrain.
Public Transport:	Arriva Medway Towns 133 from Chatham.
Parking:	On-street parking in the village.
Refreshments:	One pub in Cooling, east of the church.

After the Battle of Wrotham the rebel forces of Sir John Wyatt, gathered in Rochester, were free to advance on London, the only royalist force in the county having partly broken up and retreated. There was much support for Wyatt's stated aims of banning the marriage of Queen Mary to King Philip of Spain and ousting some of Mary's more unpopular ministers. If Wyatt had moved quickly he may have carried the day. Unfortunately for him and his men, he chose to attack Cooling Castle before marching on London.

Although with hindsight the attack on Cooling was an error, at the time it did make sense. The castle then stood on the banks of the Thames, guarding the southern flank of the estuary, and only a short distance north of the Rochester-London road. Any force there could threaten Wyatt's lines of communication back to his base of support in Kent. Wyatt may also have been counting on support from King Philip's rebellious Protestant subjects in the Spanish Netherlands. Their route to London would have been up the Thames, so the capture of Cooling Castle would have guaranteed their safe access.

Moreover Cooling Castle was owned by Lord Cobham, who was related to Wyatt by marriage and was a famously staunch Protestant. Perhaps Wyatt hoped to recruit him to the rebellion.

Cooling Church is no longer used for worship, but remains open to the public who flock here for the building's links to Charles Dickens. The writer set the opening scenes of his novel Great Expectations in and around the village.

The tombs known as Pip's Graves are those of a couple and their thirteen children who died in childhood. The graves feature prominently in Dickens' novel Great Expectations.

THE WALK

1. In Cooling find the ruined castle. The main gatehouse is difficult to miss as it dominates the road just west of the parish church. Most of the rest of the castle is now in ruins, though the moat and the East Tower remain. Modern houses have been built within the ruins as has a venue for weddings and conferences.

It was from the gatehouse towers that Lord Cobham watched as Wyatt's force advanced along the road from Rochester on the morning of 30 January 1554. The rebel army was about 4,000 men strong by this date, including about 1,000 militia men who had brought with them their modern weapons and, significantly for Cooling Castle, a cannon.

The rebel army trailed up to the church, then turned left off the road to make camp in the fields to the south. As the rebels pitched their tents in the miserable January weather, Wyatt ordered the gunners to manhandle the cannon into a position from which it could batter the walls of Cooling Castle.

2. From the castle take the lane that runs almost due south across open fields. The cannon was set up about 200 yards along this road, facing north.

Sir Thomas Wyatt took up position beside the gun. He sent a messenger to Lord Cobham demanding his surrender. From the battlements Cobham refused out of hand. It took five hours to build an emplacement, unload the ammunition and get the cannon ready to fire. Then Wyatt gave the order to fire. The gun belched forth smoke and flame – and a ball that smacked into the walls of the castle just to the right of the gatehouse.

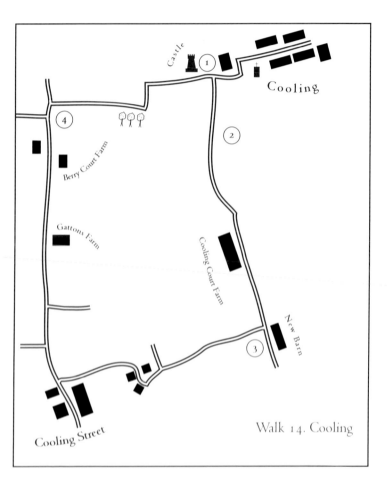

Walk 14. Cooling

Lord Cobham's flag immediately came down over the gatehouse towers and a servant slipped out from the gate. He was brought to Wyatt and asked what terms the rebels would grant for surrender. Wyatt replied that Cobham's men had to vacate the castle immediately, but were free to join the rebels or leave as they chose. Cobham

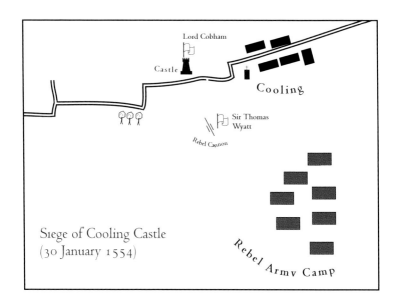

Siege of Cooling Castle
(30 January 1554)

himself would be kept a prisoner, but his life would be spared. When he heard the terms, Cobham agreed at once.

Wyatt gave orders for his own men to move into the castle. There was to be no looting, but the place was ransacked for food, ammunition and anything else of use.

2. **Continue south along the lane and so through the area where Wyatt's men were camped. Just beyond Cooling Court Farm the lane goes under a railway bridge.**

3. **Beyond the bridge a track turns off to the right, just north of New Barn Farm. Follow this track, ignoring a lane to the right to emerge on to a second surfaced lane in the hamlet of Cooling Street. Turn right to pass Gattons Farm and Berry Court Farm. The lane then meets another.**

△ The great ditch that surrounds the ruined castle. The area within the moat is large and now contains a number of private houses as well as the ruins of the castle.

▷ The ruined East Tower of Cooling Castle faces toward the church. The fire of the rebels was directed at the stretch of curtain wall, now vanished, that stood just west of this tower.

The main gatehouse of Cooling Castle still stands complete and now serves as the entrance to the largest of the various houses to lie within the ruins.

In 1554 this was the main road from London. Along this lane came riding a small group of mounted soldiers escorting a royal messenger. The messenger had come from Queen Mary herself with a simple request. Would Wyatt please tell the queen exactly what it was he wanted?

The rebellion was going well for Wyatt. He had more men than expected, the defeat at Wrotham had been turned to his advantage and now he had captured Cooling Castle. Perhaps the success went to his head. Whatever the reason, Wyatt now made a catastrophic mistake.

He told the messenger that he wanted the Tower of London turned over to him and that Queen Mary should surrender herself to him and take up residence in the Tower. After that, said Wyatt, he would decide how the country should be run. Such demands were not only astonishingly arrogant and open-ended, they went far beyond what Wyatt had told his followers that he wanted: namely to stop the marriage of Queen Mary to Philip of Spain.

As word spread through the rebel camp disquiet began. One of the first to change their minds was Lord Cobham. Instead of joining Wyatt, as he seems to have intended, Cobham at once strode off to his bedroom and refused to come out declaring that he was being kept prisoner.

4. Turn right and return to the castle along this lane.

Wyatt left some men to guard Cobham and his castle, then set off to march on London. Many in London hated the idea of the Spanish marriage, but they disliked Wyatt's terms even more and shut their gates against him. Unable to break through London's defences as easily as Cooling's the rebels were frustrated. Many began to desert and go home to Kent. Wyatt fled, but was quickly caught and taken to London for trial. He made no defence and was executed.

△ The old barn inside the catle ruins is now a venue for weddings and conferences. The grounds are adorned by old wagons and other picturesque farm machinery.

▷ From the castle the walk heads south along the lane indicated by this signpost.

The view along the lane into Cooling Street. The walk passes this way.

Set firmly to the wall of the gatehouse is a stone tablet that was put up by Lord Cobham a few weeks after the siege. It reads:

> Knouwyth that heth and schul be
> that I am mad in help of the cuntre
> In knowyng of whyche thyng
> Thys is chartre and wytnessyng.

It was a clear attempt to demonstrate his loyalty to Queen Mary. She was uncertain of Cobham's role in the rebellion and had him thrown into prison. He was soon released, however, and wisely spent the rest of his life tending his estates and staying clear of politics.

15. MAIDSTONE
1648

Distance:	5½ miles.
Terrain:	This lengthy, but undemanding walk covers well maintained footpaths along the Medway and surfaced pavements in Maidstone itself.
Public Transport:	Maidstone is served by mainline railway.
Parking:	Several car parks in the town.
Refreshments:	Numerous pubs, cafes and shops selling snacks in Maidstone. There are also two pubs in East Farleigh.

When King Charles I was captured by the Parliamentarian army in 1647 and was sent off to imprisonment on the Isle of Wight, most people thought the English Civil War was over. In fact it was only a pause.

The Scots did not like having their king locked up by the English Parliament, and many English royalists had disbanded merely due to a shortage of supplies or money, rather than a lack of fighting will or ability. Parliament had promised much during the fighting, but was unable to deliver on many of these pledges when peace came. People were unhappy and looked back to the years of peace before the war with longing. The rule of Parliament and its army was becoming unpopular. When one faction in Parliament fell out with the others, indecision and weakness gripped the government. All that was needed was a spark.

That spark came in March 1648. The garrison of Pembroke Castle had not been paid for months. When a new commander arrived with a relief force, the garrison refused to come out until they had been paid. Local royalist gentry promised that they would

△ The more southerly of the two modern bridges in central Maidstone stands at the foot of High Street on the site of the old bridge that stood here at the time of the battle. The walk starts here.

▷ The Horseway Arch opposite All Saints Church opens into the palace courtyard and stood here on the day of the battle.

A pikeman of the Civil War period. He wears bulletproof armour on his chest, groin and head as protection against gunfire from cavalry and would have used his pike to fend off attacking horsemen. Pikemen were principally defensive, but could be used to attack fortifications or enemy infantry.

be paid if they declared for the king, and they did. Within a few days all of South Wales was in uproar. In April Scotland declared war on England in the name of their imprisoned king and captured the border fortresses of Berwick and Carlisle.

In Kent the news that a major Scottish army was coming south was enough. Lord Goring, the Earl of Norwich, announced in Canterbury that he was going to declare for the king, and was at once swept along on a tide of enthusiasm. Within a week he found himself at the head of an army of royalists. Another week later and Norwich had 15,000 men under arms. Most of these men were experienced campaigners who had seen action in earlier phases of the Civil War, but they were not formed into regiments and the force lacked a command structure. If Norwich had had time to marshal his forces he would have had a powerful and potent army. But time was what Norwich did not have.

In the last week of May, Norwich learned that one of Parliament's most formidable soldiers, Sir Thomas Fairfax, was marching from London. Even worse, Fairfax had with him some

A Civil War musketeer with his gun and its rest. Battles were increasingly being settled by massed volleys of gunfire from such men.

6,000 men of the New Model Army, a superbly trained body of men equipped with the best weaponry money could buy. Norwich decided to defend the Medway, destroying the bridge at Rochester and placing garrisons at Maidstone and Aylesford, where other main roads crossed the river.

On 30 May Fairfax arrived at Rochester. He took one look at the broken bridge and the defence, then turned and marched away. Norwich guessed that Fairfax would try Aylesford next. He was wrong. Fairfax was marching on Maidstone.

THE WALK

1. In Maidstone cross to the west bank of the Medway where the A20 heads west.

It was from here that Fairfax looked across to Maidstone around noon on 1 June 1648. The town he saw was of middling size and

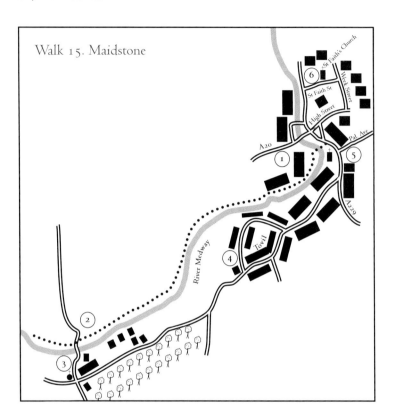

Walk 15. Maidstone

lacked any type of modern fortifications or defence. However the bridge that stood here in 1648 had been broken down by the Royalists and the far bank was lined by enemy soldiers.

Fairfax left a small group of cavalry here to watch the town's defenders, then rode off to where he had sent the bulk of his army: East Farleigh three miles upstream along the Medway.

2. Cross over the bridge to the east bank. Turn right to follow the riverside path to find a modern footbridge that crosses the

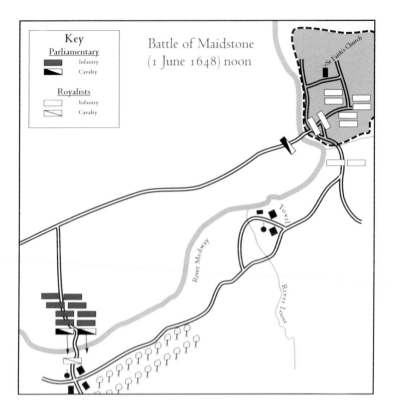

Key

Parliamentary

Infantry
Cavalry

Royalists

Infantry
Cavalry

Battle of Maidstone
(1 June 1648) noon

St Faith's Church

River Medway

Tovil

River Loose

Medway beside All Saints Church. The church is the oldest in
the town and worth a visit. Cross the footbridge, then turn
left along the Medway Valley Walk along the banks of the
river. At first the path runs through housing areas of
Maidstone, none of which were here in 1648, but it soon
leaves the built up area behind and runs along the north bank
of the river as it winds through orchards and open fields.
After a distance of almost three miles the path passes under
an ancient stone bridge at East Farleigh. Just past the bridge,

All Saints Church is the finest Perpendicular Gothic church in Kent. It stood just outside the town on the day of the battle and was one of the first buildings to fall to the Parliamentarians. The walk crosses the footbridge at the foot of the tower.

The walk crosses this modern footbridge over the Medway before leaving Maidstone. The structure stands on the site of the original ford over the river.

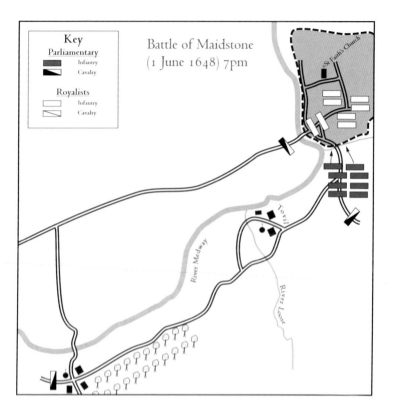

turn right between two wooden fences then right again to
meet the road beside the railway station. Turn right to reach
the bridge over the Medway.

Although Norwich knew of this bridge, he did not consider it a
serious objective for Fairfax. It was too narrow to allow the passage
of siege guns and heavier transport wagons. But Fairfax was not
intending to get his supply train over the river here, just the fighting
men of his army. Each man had enough food with him to last a

couple of days without the supply train, and tough battle-hardened soldiers could sleep in the open if necessary for a few days.

At just past noon, Fairfax gave the order to attack. Horsemen and dragoons splashed over the river, supported by gunfire from the north bank. The small royalist outpost here was quickly driven back, allowing the long columns of infantry to start streaming over the bridge. It took time to get the thousands of men over the narrow bridge, but by about 4pm Fairfax had his army on the south bank of the Medway. They formed up and began the advance on Maidstone.

3. From the bridge walk south up Station Road to the parish church. Turn left into Lower Road, the B2010 and head east. You will have an orchard on your right and the houses of East Farleigh on your left. After 300 yards the road leaves East Farleigh – and leaves behind the footpath so that it is necessary to walk on the road for the next half mile or so. Care should be taken as this is a busy road. Eventually the road reaches another cluster of houses. This is Tovil, now a suburb of Maidstone but in 1648 a separate little hamlet. Look out for the turning Burial Ground Lane on the left.

As he advanced, Fairfax sent a party of dragoons up this lane to occupy Tovil and drive out any Royalists that might be skulking there. They met with no opposition and rode through the village to rejoin the main body of their army.

4. If you wish turn left up Burial Ground Lane to follow the route of the dragoons through the what was then a little village and then on along Church Road. Alternatively continue straight up the B2010, now called Farleigh Hill. Whichever route is taken, continue along the B2010 as it

The bridge at East Farleigh seen from the south bank. The Royalists supposed to be guarding the bridge had not taken adequate precautions against attack.

Looking over East Farleigh Bridge from the north bank. The narrowness of the bridge is clear, as is the steep slope beyond. Despite these hinderances Fairfax had little difficulty forcing a passage over the river.

A Civil War dragoon. These men rode on horse
for mobility, but fought on foot. The short-
barrelled musket this man carries is a 'dragon',
hence the name dragoon.

passes through increasingly built up areas of southern
Maidstone, all of which were open fields in 1648. At the
junction with the A229 turn left. Walk north along the main
road, past the junction with another main road, Wat Tyler
Road, on the right to where Palace Avenue runs off right
beside a stream.

This stream formed the southern boundary of Maidstone in
1648. The royalists had spent the afternoon erecting barricades

The modern bridge over the stream is now a busy road junction. The Roundheads broke into the city about here, then rushed up Hayle Road beyond.

The junction of High Street and Week Street. The street fighting was particularly savage around this junction.

and other obstacles along the north bank of the stream. When Fairfax and his men arrived they found themselves facing entrenchments, sharpened stakes and other hastily erected defences, behind which were formed up hundreds of royalist musketeers and pikemen.

Although the royalists enjoyed a superiority of numbers, the men of the New Model Army were better trained, better equipped and better led. Given the narrow frontage of the action that followed, the Royalists were never able to bring their greater numbers to bear.

At 7pm Fairfax gave the order to advance. The cavalry were sent off to guard the approach roads to prevent the advance of any new cavalier force, while the infantry got on with the business of forcing the stream and getting into Maidstone.

The fighting at the stream was prolonged and bloody, but at last the Roundheads got over and began to advance into the town itself.

5. Walk north up Hayle Road, bearing right to enter High Street. Turn right along High Street where the street fighting was its most savage. Where High Street becomes King's Street, turn left along the pedestrianised Week Street. Take the second left into St Faith's Street to find St Faith's Church on your right.

This church was serving as the Royalist command headquarters in 1648 and it was to this building that many of the cavaliers retreated as dusk drew in. The church was barricaded and hurriedly fortified by the desperate men. The Roundheads first drove other fugitives north out of the town and hunted down and captured any stragglers before turning their attention to the church. One assault was pushed home, and driven off with heavy casualties before Fairfax arrived and called a halt.

At 11pm he offered surrender terms to the men holed up in the church. He offered the men their lives, though they would be imprisoned for an indefinite period. The royalists surrendered, and Fairfax was astonished when no less than a thousand men filed out of the church and into captivity. About 300 Royalists had been killed, together with about 200 Roundheads.

The fighting in Maidstone was over and the main royalist army defeated. A few other royalist forces were still in being, such as those at Rochester and Upnor, but these gave in without a fight. The Civil War really was over this time.

6. The current church is Victorian, but stands on the site of the old church and preeserves some of the ancient pillars. Old houses that stood here during the battle remain nearby. From the church walk west along St Faith's Street to a T-junction. Turn left along the A229 to return to the bridge over the Medway and the starting point of the walk.

INDEX